FEB 2 8 2010

P9-DEG-904

CULTURE SHOCK!

A Survival Guide to Customs and Etiquette

VIETNAM

Ben Engelbach

Marshall Cavendish
Editions

NAPA COUNTY LIBRARY
580 COOMBS STREET
NAPA, CA 94559

© 2017 Marshall Cavendish International (Asia) Private Limited
Text © Benjamin Englebach

Published by Marshall Cavendish Editions
An imprint of Marshall Cavendish International

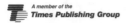
A member of the
Times Publishing Group

All rights reserved

No part of this publication may be reproduced, stored in a retrieval system or transmitted, in any form or by any means, electronic, mechanical, photocopying, recording or otherwise, without the prior permission of the copyright owner. Requests for permission should be addressed to the Publisher, Marshall Cavendish International (Asia) Private Limited, 1 New Industrial Road, Singapore 536196. Tel: (65) 6213 9300
E-mail: genref@sg.marshallcavendish.com
Website: www.marshallcavendish.com/genref

The publisher makes no representation or warranties with respect to the contents of this book, and specifically disclaims any implied warranties or merchantability or fitness for any particular purpose, and shall in no event be liable for any loss of profit or any other commercial damage, including but not limited to special, incidental, consequential, or other damages.

Other Marshall Cavendish Offices:
Marshall Cavendish Corporation. 99 White Plains Road, Tarrytown NY 10591-9001, USA • Marshall Cavendish International (Thailand) Co Ltd. 253 Asoke, 12th Flr, Sukhumvit 21 Road, Klongtoey Nua, Wattana, Bangkok 10110, Thailand • Marshall Cavendish (Malaysia) Sdn Bhd, Times Subang, Lot 46, Subang Hi-Tech Industrial Park, Batu Tiga, 40000 Shah Alam, Selangor Darul Ehsan, Malaysia

Marshall Cavendish is a registered trademark of Times Publishing Limited

National Library Board, Singapore Cataloguing-in-Publication Data

Name(s): Engelbach, Benjamin.
Title: CultureShock! Vietnam : a survival guide to customs and etiquette / Ben Engelbach.
Other title(s): Vietnam : a survival guide to customs and etiquette | Culture shock Vietnam
Description: Singapore : Marshall Cavendish Editions, [2017] | Series: Culture shock!
Identifier(s): OCN 974671695 | ISBN 978-981-4771-67-2 (paperback)
Subject(s): LCSH: Etiquette--Vietnam. | Vietnam--Social life and customs. | Vietnam--Description and travel.
Classification: DDC 959.7--dc23

Printed in Singapore by Markono Print Media Pte Ltd

Photo Credits:
All photos by the author except pages 3, 117, 172 & 179 (Chris Hocker); 8, 129, 174 & 190 (Kevin Abery); 42 (Paul Morris/unsplash.com); 43, 62, 63, 94, 134, 151, 167 & 171 (Duong Duy Thien Bao); 48 (Chinh Le Duc/ unsplash.com); 115 (RichardX/pixabay.com); 140: Danang (Phua Li Ling); 161 (Tommy Southgate); 184 (Hoang Nguyen); and 247 (Mohammed Sami). • Cover photo by Noi Ha Tran

All illustrations by TRIGG

PREFACE

Dear Reader:

You know how life works: It pulls us around the dance floor and pushes us into unexpected corners of it. After all, look what happened to you. One thing led to the next, and you ended up in Vietnam. Maybe you were reassigned to your company's Hanoi branch. Or maybe your wife was reassigned to Hanoi and now she's dragging you across the Pacific with her. Either way, welcome abroad.

No matter what your backstory is, you'll be an outsider in Vietnam, and outsiders tend to be clueless. But that's OK—that can be fixed. What follows is my full report, compiled over the course of what's now been a year in this hot, strange little country.

Some context: I live and work in the capital of Hanoi, but did my due diligence by flying down to Ho Chi Minh City (the urbanity formerly known as Saigon) to spend two weeks wandering through the markets and eating enough food to feed an army. Most expats in Vietnam end up getting sucked in by the tractor beams of one of these two big cities, which is why I name-check them so often, and have devoted a substantial percentage of my word count to demarcating their differences. If you happen to be moving to Danang or Haiphong, don't fret—the information that follows holds true for you too.

By this point in my tour of duty I've cleared a few of the hurdles you're about to run into, which is why I think this book will be a useful read. I'm not a Communist cheerleader, nor do I have a tour to sell—I'm here to give you the unfiltered take on the place. I'll tell you what will treat you well and

ABOUT THE SERIES

Culture shock is a state of disorientation that can come over anyone who has been thrust into unknown surroundings, away from one's comfort zone. *CultureShock!* is a series of trusted and reputed guides which has, for decades, been helping expatriates and long-term visitors to cushion the impact of culture shock whenever they move to a new country.

Written by people who have lived in the country and experienced culture shock themselves, the authors share all the information necessary for anyone to cope with these feelings of disorientation more effectively. The guides are written in a style that is easy to read and cover a range of topics that will arm readers with enough advice, hints and tips to make their lives as normal as possible again.

Each book is structured in the same manner. It begins with the first impressions that visitors will have of that city or country. To understand a culture, one must first understand the people—where they came from, who they are, the values and traditions they live by, as well as their customs and etiquette. This is covered in the first half of the book.

Then on with the practical aspects—how to settle in with the greatest of ease. Authors walk readers through how to find accommodation, get the utilities and telecommunications up and running, enrol the children in school and keep in the pink of health. But that's not all. Once the essentials are out of the way, venture out and try the food, enjoy more of the culture and travel to other areas. Then be immersed in the language of the country before discovering more about the business side of things.

To round off, snippets of information are offered before readers are 'tested' on customs and etiquette. Useful words and phrases, a comprehensive resource guide and list of books for further research are also included for easy reference.

CONTENTS

what you'll have to struggle through. Between geographical immersion and interviews with both Vietnamese locals and fellow expats, I think I managed to check all the boxes for you. You'll be duly warned of the flower-killing smog, the nuclear-hot sun, the crush of traffic, and the ceaseless rain. But you'll also turn the last page itching for a *banh mi* sandwich with a *ca phe trung* (egg coffee).

As an expat you'll be both a guest and an ambassador. You'll have to study and infiltrate the culture like a sleeper agent. It'll take some work—but it's fun work. Vietnam has a sort of unique magnetism that keeps most people here long after their initial end-dates. And when they do leave, you'll see a lot of them again; nearly every expat is subject to the Vietnamese boomerang effect.

Another thing about life is that it's never perfect. You'll probably suffer through a few small disasters while you're here, and that's when your mind will start to whisper that what you hoped would be an adventure was actually a mistake, and that this country and everyone in it is out to get you.

But that's not really true. Everything that happens here is just a result of Vietnam being itself, and the Vietnamese you encounter are people just like you, who are just getting by. And every baffling inconvenience is part of the authentic experience.

And that's what you came here for, right?

Ben Engelbach
Hanoi
1 April 2017

ACKNOWLEDGEMENTS

I have a legion of Vietnamese friends and fellow expats to thank for their assistance on this project. I owe you all a deep debt for the long stretches of time you spent sitting across from me, the clueless one, in a café and answering an unholy amount of questions. You're welcome to a beer (or three) next time I see you in Hanoi.

I also have to mention my students, the dozens and dozens of you, who I've been with in the classroom for the better part of a year. Your energy and curiosity have made my job feel more like a hangout, or maybe like hosting a talk show, and our conversations have given me insights into Vietnam's culture and inner workings that I'd have been hard-pressed to chase down elsewhere. Thanks to all of your expertise, I've become a pseudo-know it all on the subject of Vietnam (the guy at the bar who starts sentences with "Well, actually...").

Noi Ha Tran, Tommy Southgate, Chris Hocker, Kevin Abery, Hoang Nguyen, Duong Duy Thien Bao and Mohammed Sami contributed photographs to this project, and elevated it in a way that I wouldn't have been able to, even if I were shooting with the world's best camera.

And finally, special thanks must go to two people: John Bocskay, author of *Culture Shock! Korea*, who recommended me for this book, and Rachel Heng of Marshall Cavendish for taking me on board.

And of course, any errors, whether they be factual ones or errors with lingual transcriptions, should be attributed to me and me alone.

AUTHOR'S NOTE

It's worth mentioning that we'll be using the Westernized names of Vietnamese locations in this book. For example, in the Vietnamese language, the city of Hanoi is written as Hà Nội (each syllable is given its own word, and tone markers are visible above the letters). But we'll use the international style, which combines the syllables together and removes the tone markers, resulting in "Hanoi".

The exceptions are in Chapter 8: Languages and parts of the Glossary and Resource Guide where relevant.

FIRST IMPRESSIONS

Bizarre travel plans are dancing lessons from God.

— Kurt Vonnegut, writer

Let's start with the good news: I'll be surprised if you don't love Vietnam.

Gallons of ink have been spilled describing the country's charm and beauty, and those may well be the reasons you board the plane for the East. And you'll find what you came for. After a half-decade of criss-crossing Asia, I can put my hand on the Bible and say that Vietnam's landscapes, bays, and mountain ranges are among the best on the continent.

If it's adventure you seek, you can be on a motorbike and out of the city a few hours after your plane lands. If you end up staying in-country for a while, you'll find yourself leaning back at a lakefront *bia hoi*, holding a 50-cent mug of beer as you realize that you're living in a paradise. The expat consensus is so unanimous that it verges on propaganda; I haven't talked to anyone who doesn't like living here.

Now that the good news is out of the way, let's get to the dirt. Just because Vietnam rides high in the approval polls doesn't mean your stay here will be one long, sunlit travel montage. It'll do you well to remember that this country is still a very real place. Hopefully this will prevent you from getting off the plane in Hanoi or Ho Chi Minh City (that's what they're calling Saigon these days) and finding yourself… disappointed.

Because that's what happened to me. I'd heard nothing but glorious legends told of Vietnam, which led to my expectations being wildly miscalibrated. The consequence of buying into the hype was that my first 72 hours in Hanoi

Workers in the rice fields, circa 2016.

ended up being the opposite of a honeymoon period, whatever that is.

As promised, I did see the French mansions and the broad, shady lanes when I first got here. But I soon internalized that the country is more than just a pretty postcard you can walk around in; it's actually a real place, with grit and chaos being two of its defining characteristics. These new realities quickly threatened to outweigh its Instagram potential.

Visit Vietnam, and you're visiting another planet — and the past as well. The country is still pushing through the adolescent phase of its development, after having its progress blunted by a famously turbulent (that's putting it mildly) 20th century.

The highway heading into Hanoi from Noi Bai International Airport cuts across a sprawl of rice paddies, where workers in those iconic rice hats toil away as if in a staged tableau. That's the pretty side of living in the past. But there's a practical side, too. There have been a few times when I've had to slow my motorbike to navigate around a parade of cows being force-marched along the median by a farmer. I swerved wide to get around the herd—and had to brake quickly so I wouldn't T-bone one of them. It had been trying to escape from the farmer, who was trying to smack it with a switch.

You'll probably spend your first few days in one of Vietnam's two biggest cities (Hanoi or Saigon). Now, on Planet Earth we have quiet cities, and we have chaotic ones. Guess what kind Vietnam has?

The urban streets are jagged, crumbling and altogether too narrow to accommodate the endless surge of motorbikes that rumble over them every day. Do you need to go somewhere? Well, I've got some bad news for you. Traffic isn't a joke—the city turns itself inside out during morning and evening rush hours. If you're driving, prepare yourself for a slow, grinding game of land warfare as you battle for every inch. The only thing worse than loitering away your existence in gridlock is not doing so — because bikers are free to shoot around as fast as they want (for some reason, they ride like they're being chased by an F-16) wherever they want (almost invariably, this means going the wrong way down a

one-way). Stay sharp, because they will hit you. My friend was knocked down on her second day here. She got off pretty easy — just a scrape — but you may not be so fortunate. I have other friends who have ended up staying a night or two in the hospital after suffering collisions of their own. Best to always err on the cautious side.

There's also the air quality in town. It is — how shall we put this diplomatically — less than optimal. On the day of this writing, Hanoi had literally become the most-polluted major city in the world (at least for a few hours), beating out perennial champ Beijing. By the time rush hour hits, the air has become superheated by bike and bus exhaust (at the first chance you get, buy a surgical mask from a roadside vendor). More smoke rises at night, as the locals burn trash piles in the gutter.

Perhaps keen to suffer from as many kinds of pollution as possible, Hanoi has added noise pollution to the mix, too. From around 4pm each day, a system of war-era loudspeakers blare public service announcements and patriotic anthems for an hour, sometimes two (bring noise-cancelling headphones). What's with the noise? Isn't it 2017, and doesn't Vietnam have the Internet for communication?

That it does, but Vietnamese officials still don't see what all the fuss over the World Wide Web is all about — (maybe they think it's a passing fad?) — and still insist that a high-decibel public broadcast system is the best way to spread information. I wish you the best of luck if you're trying to catch a power nap.

And when you wake up with a dry mouth, don't drink the tap water, not unless you want to spend your first day camped out within sprinting radius of the hotel bathroom. While we're on the subject of stomachaches, that reminds me — did you

The First Night

I found some notes from my first day in Hanoi while I was prepping for this book. After landing, despite reeling from the one-two punch of culture shock and jet lag, my friend and I rallied and headed to the Night Market for dinner.

The Night Market is written as a proper noun because it's a weekly festival in the city. Every Friday, Saturday, and Sunday night, the city closes off a half-dozen streets in Hanoi's Old Quarter so vendors can sell T-shirts and scarves and all the other "I've-been-to-Vietnam" souvenirs. You do your shopping, or just sit on one of the stools that the restaurants have set up outside in the night air.

It's sort of an anarchical experience, with bright lights strobing and locals hollering and bumping into you… and you shouldn't miss it.

This is what I wrote:

• Sat in the cab for 20 minutes only to travel two blocks. Too many bikes and carts and people; no discernible traffic laws; transportation is a cutthroat, move-or-die enterprise. Will never take a taxi to the night market (or through the city centre?) again.

• Pretty eclectic cuisine — frog legs, bok choy, fish (with bones in it), etc.

• Live bands on the street really energize the whole scene, but also make it too loud to really talk to each other.

• Best to hold it. Restaurant bathroom is akin to what I've seen in bus stations in America, except these ones have no toilet paper and take up the square footage of a broom closet.

• Unimaginatively-named beer. Hanoi's local brew is simply called "Hanoi". Saw a few bottles of "Saigon" as well.

• Finishing on a positive note, the combined price of the meal and taxi was cheap, US$3. (We're paying 1950s prices for everything here.)

forget to wash your hands before you ate? Then you've got something in common with the cooks; they probably didn't wash their hands before preparing your food.

Also, if you have a foreign face, be prepared to pay double the listed price of an item, or to receive incorrect change via sleight of hand. And I hope you like asking for things, because you'll have to do it two or three times in events when there's no financial incentive for the service staff involved.

These needling, startling frustrations go a little way

toward explaining why I, a Westerner blindly accustomed to convenience, had to acquire my taste for urban Vietnam. My inaugural chipper Facebook posts were all lies; what really happened was that I spent my first nights here sitting on a dirty plastic chair in a *banh cuon* restaurant—with rats running between my feet, twitching tails the width of telephone cables—while I ruminated darkly over the chain of events that led me here.

Now. Your perception could be completely different. You might get here and love it straight away.

But if you walk off the plane and get hit with culture shock like I did, hang tough. The clouds will part (that promise is metaphorical; the smog cover isn't going anywhere), and you'll remember what I said at the start of this chapter—that Vietnam is as gorgeous, alluring, and charming as advertised. It's a strange maze to navigate, but you can get through it. And after a while, you won't even notice the cows.

A man moves through a thin alley in Saigon. (Photo credit: Kevin Abery)

FIRST IMPRESSIONS: SAIGON

Since I live in the capital, I imagine that makes me an honorary Hanoian. But I realize that many of you will be moving to Ho Chi Minh City. It's the largest city in Vietnam, the former capital of the now-vanquished Republic of South Vietnam (more on that later), as well as the country's primary international business outpost.

So, just for you, I flew down south to do some recon. My flight was delayed, and by the time I got on to the bus into the city centre it was 5pm. And every day at that time, I have a Pavlovian anxiety attack — in Hanoi, 5pm is the end of the world. Evening traffic is so thick that the city grinds to an ugly, shuddering halt. The only way you're getting anywhere in less than an hour is by helicopter.

Saigon was definitely busy, but while I was on the airport bus, I still had the sensation of slow, consistent motion. I realized that it was because parts of the city were developed more recently, which means the roads are wider. I got the impression of space and manoeuvrability. It was as if dimensions that I'd been subconsciously accustomed to for the past six months had been stretched out by the hands of a giant.

The variety of restaurants and street food in Saigon is such that I'd need the rest of my life, and yours too, to sample everything. There are glass storefronts and smoky, high-dollar restaurants and corporate towers aplenty. When you're downtown, you can sense the money in a way that you don't in Hanoi. And being more cosmopolitan, Saigon therefore carries the impersonal vibe you'd expect (the population went from starving to comfortably aloof in just a few decades).

In District 1, where Google Images seems to have pulled all of its "Saigon" search results from, the city fairly gleams with eternal celebration, what with its towers and golden halls standing proudly on the Saigon River. Saigon, like New York City and Shanghai, is one of those cities that feels so much like a capital—and yet isn't one (anymore). It's still Vietnam, but after seeing the North, it feels like a Vietnam set up in an alternate universe.

Of course, as you drift away from the bulls' eye of the city centre and explore the outer rings, you'll see that Saigon is still rough and tumble, still the real Vietnam. There are the givens—the crumbling sidewalks, the shady (literally and

Saigon or Ho Chi Minh?

Officially, it's Ho Chi Minh City. But that was a top-down name change put into effect by the victorious political elite in the postwar period.

What do the people call it? The locals laughed at me for even asking—to them, it's Saigon. It's been called Saigon since the colonial French named it such in 1860 (the city had gone by Gia Dinh prior to that). The locals live in Saigon, they're Saigonese, and they eat Saigonese food. "Saigon" rolls off the tongue easier, too—"Ho Chi Minh City" is an unwieldly jumble of syllables, and it feels like it takes an hour to say.

figuratively) alleys, and streetside bike repair operations.

One disappointment: There's a dearth of *bia hoi* (cheap beer gardens, common to the North) down there, so I had to look a little harder for my first cheap buzz after my day trek through the streets.

It's hard to form an inclusive opinion on this country without walking through both its capital and its largest city, the two weights that keep the nation anchored in the top and bottom. Hanoi is a straight, pure shot of all that is and has been Vietnam. It's in your face, and doesn't pander. Saigon? It's the antidote some expats might need after doing time up in the North. I expect I'd have taken more kindly to Vietnam if I'd eased into it by using Saigon as a "gateway" city.

It's all about what you're looking for.

CHAPTER 2

OVERVIEW
OF LAND
AND HISTORY

> ❝History repeats itself.
> Historians repeat each other.❞

—Philip Guedalla, barrister and writer

GEOGRAPHY

Vietnam is a Southeast Asian country that immediately borders Laos, Cambodia, and China. It forms the eastern edge of the Indochinese Peninsula, and it kind of looks like an "S" if you squint a little.

From top to bottom, Vietnam stretches for more than 1,000 miles, a distance that creates a considerable weather differential between the North and the South.

Much of Vietnam is either hilly, forested, or both. The two main rivers are the Red River Delta in the North and the larger Mekong Delta in the South. The northern half of the country holds more mountains than the South does.

WEATHER AND SEASONS

Northern Vietnam experiences all four seasons, though winter is pretty mild (a jacket should keep you warm enough). The South languishes under a tropical sun year-round, and it only has two seasons: Wet and dry.

The one national constant is rain.

Those who have seen the film *Forrest Gump* may recall that Vietnam receives far more than what can be considered a fair amount of it, and the rainy season generally lasts from approximately May to October—though don't expect the rain to respect this time frame exactly. It falls when it pleases. If you didn't pack an umbrella, then pick one up when you get here, and while you're at it, buy a poncho to stash in your motorbike. As a consequence of the incessant rain, Vietnam also has to deal with periodic flash floods and landslides. You'll be safe from them in the cities, but there will still be times where you'll have to drive yourself up a shallow river that had been a street earlier that day.

As you might expect, Vietnamese winters are mild. Outside the mountaintops, you won't find any snow, what with the country's subtropical climate. Autumn and spring will be appropriately mild, as well.

But as you also might expect, summer in Vietnam is a merciless affair that feels like someone left a giant blast

Yes, It Is Hot Enough For Me, Thanks

The day summer fully kicked in, I arrived at work completely soaked from the commute, my skin slick as a seal's and my work shirt translucent with sweat. This was my "never again" moment, and for the rest of the summer I took to wearing a T-shirt for the drive and changing into my work clothes when I got to the office.

Beauty is Pain

You are riding across the city, existing in a latent state of misery as you catch the full beam of the summer sun. A T-shirt is the most you'd ever wear on a day like today; another layer would bring on heatstroke. So why are half of the bikers sharing the road with you bundled up like hikers on Everest?

Those are the Vietnamese women. They're willing to suffer considerable discomfort to protect their skin from the sun. No matter how high the mercury rises, they still ride their motorbikes while clad in gloves, hooded jackets, sunglasses and face masks, leaving not an inch of skin exposed. It makes me think that whoever manufactures Hazmat suits should set up shop here.

This won't sound too crazy if you've been around Asia a little bit. From Japan to South Korea and all the way down to Southeast Asia, this region places a premium on keeping one's visage pale and unblemished, especially for women.

---

furnace open. Even up north in Hanoi, the temperatures can crack 40 degrees Celsius (104 Fahrenheit). Running the air conditioner will cool you down at the same time it burns your cash. My electricity bill for June converted out to over US$100 — easily my biggest expense outside of rent itself. After that, I bought a fan and just aimed it at wherever I was sitting at home, and cut the next month's bill in half.

You'll likely get around Vietnam on a motorbike, and all I can tell you is that you should prepare for the unpleasant experience of sitting in open-air traffic during the summer months. Trapped in gridlock with the sun beating down on you, while you bake in the hot engine wash radiating out from the other vehicles around you, your daily commute becomes a test of fortitude.

POLITICAL GEOGRAPHY

Vietnam takes up an area of land slightly greater than that of the US state of New Mexico, and that land itself is split into 58 provinces and five centrally-governed municipalities.

Those state-run municipalities are the cities of Hanoi, Ho Chi Minh City, Can Tho, Danang, and Haiphong, along with their surroundings. The five municipalities are separated into districts of their own (some rural, others urban), and each district is made up of wards. The provinces are further split into districts (*huyen*), which are in turn divided into district-level towns. Vietnamese provinces are each governed by their own People's Council, made up of councillors elected by the province's inhabitants. These provincial governments defer to the central government—which controls the five government municipalities.

The "big two" cities, Hanoi and Saigon, are split into districts. In Hanoi, they're given names. (I live in Tay Ho

---

Addresses

An alley sign in Hanoi.

Your address in Vietnam could be a few degrees more complex than what you're used to in the West. This is because of the alley system.

For example, to reach my house, you follow the main road to alley 124. Then you turn onto sub-alley 22, before finally turning into sub-sub-alley 16. How do you even write that? You go fractional, like this: 124/22/16.

Some alleys and roads are unmarked, so budget in extra time if you're going to be hunting down a destination using the address alone.

If you're having something shipped from overseas, it's a wise move to splurge on a professional delivery service such as DHL. I've heard horror stories of packages being rifled through at Customs and finally arriving with missing items, if they arrived at all.

Another option is having visiting friends "smuggle" goods into the country for you. Case in point, I bought some shoes online (if you're especially tall or have got big feet, abandon all hope now of finding your shoe size in Vietnam) and had them shipped to my buddy's house in America. When he came over for a vacation, he pulled double-duty as my personal courier and delivered the shoes to me.

District, for example). Saigon, being so expansive, has so many districts that some have been named, while the rest are just numbered.

WILDLIFE

As far as Vietnam's animal kingdom goes, you won't have much to worry about. Though if you're planning on living in a city (which you most likely are) and you don't like rats, then I've got some bad news for you. They'll be everywhere — in the restaurants, in the gutters, and darting out in front of your bike. Many families raise chickens in their yards, and just before dawn the chickens will start clucking and wake up the dogs, who will bark and wake you up. Good morning!

If you find yourself heading outside the city, the wildlife won't be much of a concern. Vietnam's animals are generally afraid of the humans, and not the other way around. Vietnamese poachers are waging a steady war on a number of endangered species, including rhinos and elephants.

HISTORY

Due to Vietnam's prolonged, bloody cameo on the world stage during the 1960s and 1970s, we have more passing knowledge of the nation than we do of, say, Cambodia or Laos. But there's a lot more to Vietnamese history than "The Resistance War Against America," as it's called here.

What follows is a quick sprint through Vietnam's story that will give some context for when you get over here.

The Beginning

Archeological evidence places the first human inhabitants of Vietnam as early as 500,000 years ago. But the first culture we'll talk about is the Dong Sun, who are remembered for cultivating rice and sailing dugout canoes through the Red River Delta (where Hanoi now sits). They also became quite adept at casting bronze drums, which have been found all around the region, including up in southern China.

The Dong Sun emerged sometime around 300 BC. A century later they were conquered by southward-pressing Chinese forces, who stuck around for almost a full millennium and forced Vietnamese leaders and officials to study the Chinese customs, language and culture.

During China's stay, they crushed every revolt that arose (for a good read, look up the Trung sisters' rebellion). While these periodic insurrections were going on, various regions of faraway southern Vietnam were briefly folded into Cambodian and Hindi kingdoms. It wasn't until the collapse of China's

Tang Dynasty that the Vietnamese were able to deal their rulers a big loss. A new uprising culminated in a huge battle on the Bach Dang River in AD 938 that finally sent the Chinese forces home.

A newly independent Vietnam then proceeded to repulse attacks from a barrage of foreign powers, from the Khmer to the Mongols to the Chinese (again), establishing a motif that has held all the way up to the modern era. Of course, good luck doesn't last forever, and the Chinese again conquered Vietnam at the start of the 1400s, only to be sent packing (again) during the Lam Son Uprising, which concluded in 1428.

With all foreign invaders having lost heart, Vietnam then went through a period on infighting that would last throughout the 17th and 18th centuries. The long country was essentially divided in half during this time, with the Trinh lords in the North repeatedly trying and failing to extract submission from the Nguyen family, a rebellious, irreverent faction who controlled the South. Eventually the two sides reached a stalemate, and Vietnam remained fragmented until the French managed to add the nation to their empire.

Enter the West

Vietnam's first considerable Western influence came in the form of Portuguese traders who landed at Danang in 1516. They brought with them the Catholic faith, which was permitted to spread within the country for a good few centuries until the Vietnamese Mandarins began to see it as a threat to Confucianism and executed a number of missionaries and converts. This backlash gave the French an excuse to attack Danang and a few other coastal cities, thus beginning a slow, messy conquest of Vietnam.

Soon enough, France gained enough power to control the entirety of the country. Exerting control via a string of puppet emperors in the Imperial Court in Hue, the French were able to maintain control over "French Indochina" until the Japanese overran the area during World War II (France would regain control after the war ended).

While ambitious in developing local infrastructure, the French treated their subjects without much respect. Native labourers were underpaid, underfed and overtaxed, and Vietnamese resentment simmered and seethed through the French dominion. As is the way of the subjugated, the Vietnamese wanted their independence — and their nation — back.

The 20th century was a time of global shifts and upheaval. Nations and empires rose and fell apart. This time of flux and chaos would provide an opportune break for the Vietnamese. It just so happened that one of their own, a man who lived abroad and went by the name Quoc, was about to give his countrymen an idea to rally behind.

The Man of Many Names

After leaving Vietnam, Quoc travelled and worked in Europe and America. A particularly galvanizing experience for him came when he lived in France following World War I. At that time, Quoc was still going by his Confucian name, Thanh.

Thanh, then in his late 20s, joined a Vietnamese nationalist group based in Paris, and they modelled a manifesto of self-determination after the US's Declaration of Independence. At the Versailles Peace Talks, Thanh attempted to get the attention of the American delegation and President Woodrow Wilson, hoping to gain their assistance in removing French colonial rule. He was ignored.

After this, he became known as Nguyen Ai Quoc (a name meaning "Nguyen the Patriot") and eventually wound up studying Marxist principles in Russia for a time in the pre-World War II period. He also spent the run-up to World War II living in Thailand and China, all the while fostering and monitoring the Vietnamese Communist movement from afar.

All of this is relevant because you've probably heard of Quoc before. He was born in 1890 as Nguyen Sinh Cung, received his Confucian name (Thanh) at age 10, and by 1940 he'd begun calling himself Ho Chi Minh.

"Ho" is a Vietnamese surname. "Chi Minh" can be translated as "with the will of light." Uncle Ho, as he's known here, is all over the country—on murals and on every piece of currency.

Final Push for Independence

1941 brought war to the globe and also brought Ho Chi Minh back home. He returned to Vietnam that year to direct the resistance movement against the Japanese Occupation. Said resistance, the Viet Minh, was supported by the US's Office of Strategic Service, as at that point they were on the same side of the Allies vs. Axis fight.

That particular fight ended in 1945 with the surrender of Japan. But Vietnam still had 30 bloody years of history ahead of it before it could finally call itself a unified and independent nation.

Attaining this status was Ho Chi Minh's ultimate goal. His method for getting there was to harness the people's willpower and nationalism, and focus it under the Communist standard.

One of Ho's first victories following the end of World War II was convincing Vietnam's then-puppet emperor, Bao Dai, to abdicate his throne in favour of the Viet Minh independence movement. This was the de facto blessing that put Ho Chi Minh in the driver's seat of Vietnam's destiny. Having all but eliminated anti-Communist forces in North Vietnam, Ho then set up a provisional government, with himself at the head.

In September 1945, he famously rallied a crowd in Hanoi's Ba Dinh Square and issued a declaration of Vietnamese independence from France, while simultaneously proclaiming the birth of Democratic Republic of Vietnam (the official name for what everyone called "North Vietnam").

Just as he had during his ill-fated appeal in Versailles, he wrote to the American State Department to seek formal recognition and aid for his new nation. Again, he received no response.

Ho and his Viet Minh then set about handling the French problem, as the Europeans had returned to their old colony in late 1945 to "reclaim our inheritance", as one general put it.

But they never could quite reclaim it. Ho and his forces fled Hanoi as the French overran it in 1946, but continued to harass and humiliate their invaders via guerilla warfare tactics for nearly a decade, keeping true sovereignty out of European reach. The Viet Minh finally solved their French problem in 1954 with their victory in the Battle of Dien Bien Phu—a loss that became the last straw for an exhausted and frustrated France.

During the battle Vietnamese forces, bearing arms supplied to them by their comrade nations of Russia, China and East Germany, pulled heavy artillery pieces and anti-aircraft guns up muddy slopes in order to rain heavy fire down on the French, who'd fortified the valley of Dien Bien Phu. This manoeuvre shocked the enemy, who had thought themselves safe in a valley surrounded by high, seemingly inaccessible peaks. After suffering through a two-month siege, the Europeans surrendered.

Cold War Battlefront

Their stunning defeat at Dien Bien Phu added France to the long list of foreign powers who have tried and failed to break the will of Vietnam—and they weren't going to be the last country on that list. Because the Americans, surely never ones to stay at home, were about to make their own power play in Indochina.

However, before the US showed up, there was the Geneva Conference. This international summit commenced immediately after the Battle of Dien Bien Phu. The conference's two purposes were to discuss still-unresolved issues from the Korean War, and to ascertain how to best proceed with the tumultuous situation in Vietnam.

The talks resulted in a French agreement to withdraw its troops from North Vietnam. It was also decided that Vietnam would be split along the 17th parallel. This arrangement was planned to last until a vote could be held determining the government of a reunified Vietnam.

Just as had been the case on the Korean peninsula, the two Vietnams both picked up foreign sponsors as the newly-crowned superpowers of the USA and the USSR scrapped for influence in the hemisphere. The Communist governments of Soviet Russia and China backed the government to the North, while the Americans provided support and advisors to the "democratic" government in the South. The quote marks will make sense if you've ever caught a History Channel documentary about the Vietnam War, during which you might've learned about Ngo Dinh Diem, a politician who became the leader of the South Vietnam.

In 1955, Diem seized power in a rigged referendum and proclaimed himself president. While he was a Catholic and a staunch anti-Communist, he nevertheless governed much like the tyrants whose ideology he rejected. Political opponents could be censored, banned from assembling, jailed or executed.

In the meantime, Ho Chi Minh returned to Hanoi and his government also began to cement their grip on power. They arrested, imprisoned and executed potential dissidents. Ho called on Diem to hold the agreed-upon national elections. Diem, fearing he'd lose a popularity contest to Ho, refused.

This political avenue exhausted, Ho and his Viet Minh once again decided to go to guns in a bid to reunify the country. Hanoi created the National Liberation Front (NLF) in 1960, and while you might not have heard of the NLF, you probably have heard of the Viet Cong, who were the NLF's military arm. VC militia, many of whom had previously lived in the South, began funnelling down the country on the Ho Chi Minh Trail to push back the South Vietnamese Army. This army, shorthanded as ARVN (Army of the Republic of South Vietnam) quickly lost ground to the northern forces.

By 1963 Ngo Dinh Diem had fallen out of favour with his people, and his brutal crackdowns on protests did little to prop up his image—and no one was impressed with his inability to hold back the communist tide rolling down from the North. Seen as an incompetent quasi-dictator, he was assassinated in 1963 in a military coup backed by his American counterpart, John F. Kennedy.

Somewhat coincidentally, Kennedy would himself be assassinated a mere three weeks after Diem. And his successor, Lyndon Johnson, would be the man who first committed American combat troops to Vietnam.

"The" War

This is the part they told you about in school. What the West calls The Vietnam War more or less kicked off in 1965, when elements of the US military first arrived in the country. By that point, North Vietnamese Army (NVA) regulars were pouring south along with the Viet Cong militia, and the government in Saigon seemed to be living out its last days.

American forces were under orders from Washington to keep a Communist "domino" from falling in Vietnam, and to "contain" Communist influence there. They were there on the authority of the Gulf of Tonkin Resolution, a US Congressional response to a report from sailors on the USS Maddox, who claimed they were fired on without provocation by a North Vietnamese torpedo boat while off the coast of Vietnam. But in 2005, newly declassified papers revealed that the USS Maddox had actually fired first, which in effect reduced the US's official rationale for involvement in Vietnam into a falsehood.

For all its blood spilled and lives lost, the Vietnam War was actually termed an "engagement" — war was never officially declared. South Korea, Australia, Thailand, New Zealand and the Philippines also contributed varying numbers of troops to the fight.

It was a misconception that Uncle Ho was a Communist acolyte who'd drunk the Russian Kool-Aid, and was therefore desperate battling to impose the Soviet way on his country. The reality was that Ho's pleas for Western assistance in his push for independence had been ignored. The Soviets, on the other hand, were more than willing to provide the arms he'd need for the fight.

Ho would later say, "It was patriotism, not communism, that inspired me." It certainly helped his recruitment process

Tourists look at the anti-war posters on display in Saigon's War Remnants Museum.

that it was easy for him to frame the American forces as invaders and "imperialists", and the South Vietnamese as their sellout collaborators.

Showdown

The fight would rage longer than World War II did, as the two sides punched and counterpunched. The rounds of the brawl are well-known. There was Operation Rolling Thunder, the three-year US bombing campaign on the North. This phase of the war ended up spilling over into Cambodia and Laos as the US tried to cut off Communist supply lines and prop up flagging Southern morale.

These objectives ultimately went unfulfilled, despite the fact the Americans ended up dropping twice as many bombs during this conflict than they had in World War II. The Ho Chi Minh trail was a living, shifting thing that simply regenerated and moved whenever it was smashed. Troops and supplies just kept on flowing south.

But 1968 was when the North kicked the war into high gear with an assault on US-operated Khe Sanh Combat Base. Khe Sanh turned into a 77-day siege and was the biggest single battle of the war. And while the North was repulsed, it later turned out that their failure was both foreseen and intended. Khe Sanh was a mirage and a distraction from the NVA's preparations for its real attack: The Tet Offensive.

Tet is the Vietnamese New Year and the country's most important festival, and the North used the cover of the holiday to stage an all-out attack on the South. (For an American equivalent of a Tet Offensive, imagine waking up on Christmas morning to see tanks and soldiers outside your bedroom window.) Violating their own holiday ceasefire, the NVA simultaneously assaulted over one hundred targets in South Vietnam. The US launched a scorched-earth counterattack in response, shelling a number of towns and cities — many of which housed civilians — in hopes of beating back the NVA.

Ultimately, the North lost that round — but only militarily speaking. That idea doesn't make much sense until you see the footage of the Viet Cong occupying the courtyard of the US Embassy in Saigon. Never mind that they were only on the

US military equipment on display in the courtyard of Saigon's War Remnants Museum.

grounds for six hours before being gunned down—American voters, watching the evening news, had already seen evidence of a successful enemy attack. If anything, it was an image that underscored the ideas of defeat and vulnerability.

Tet would end up being a huge psychological victory for North as it showed the Americans and the South Vietnamese as being unprepared for the Communists' manoeuvres. Tet is a singular encapsulation how the entire war played out: the North won the war by continually losing it. They were unafraid of the cost of the victory, and they just kept coming.

This is also to say nothing of other PR disasters such as the My Lai massacre, when US Army troops executed a village of several hundred South Vietnamese in frustration after coming up empty-handed on a search-and-destroy mission for Viet Cong.

In 1972, US President Richard Nixon authorized the Operation Linebacker bombing raids on North Vietnam that hit supply and logistical targets. Some view the Linebacker blasts as key factors in hastening Hanoi's approach to the negotiating table. But while they produced measured results, they only delayed the war's denouement. The NVA, though slowed, continued to move south.

Faced with a seemingly invincible enemy and the task of continually selling an unpopular war to a sceptical (and that's putting it mildly) American public, the US finally bowed out in 1973 with the signing of the Paris Peace Accords. South Vietnam's destiny was now in its own hands.

The North Vietnamese then violated the ceasefire mandated by the Peace Accords and laid siege to the South. Lacking any outside assistance, South Vietnam folded relatively quickly. On 30 April 1975, the North Vietnamese overran Saigon. American helicopters frantically ferried troops and South Vietnamese out to aircraft carriers waiting off the coast as the city collapsed around them. At noon, a North Vietnamese tank literally overran the gates of the Independence Palace, the wartime workplace of the South Vietnamese government. General Duong Van Minh—the same man who had taken over South Vietnam in 1963 after purging of Duong Van Min—emerged from the palace and formally surrendered to the North's Colonel Bui Tin.

Vietnam was officially reunified in July 1976, but Uncle Ho never saw the culmination of his great campaign. He had passed away in 1969, six years before the war's end. In memory of the Vietnamese leader, Saigon was renamed Ho Chi Minh City. Today, his embalmed body lies in a grand mausoleum in Hanoi's Ba Dinh Square, the place where he'd once declared Vietnamese independence.

The Ho Chi Minh Mausoleum in Hanoi's Ba Dinh Square.

The Price Paid

Said independence came at a heavy human cost. Counting both sides, anywhere from 700,000 to 1.6 million Vietnamese troops and guerillas died in the conflict. This is to say nothing of the several million civilians who were caught in the crossfire. By comparison, America would check out of the conflict with 58,000 dead.

But the arithmetic of casualties simply didn't apply to this war. As Ho Chi Minh would say, "You will kill 10 of our men, and we will kill one of yours, and in the end it will be you who tire of it."

One of my coworkers is from a village outside of Hanoi, and she said there's an old woman who lives on her road. The old woman is now at the end of her life and she has no children; all eight of her sons died fighting against the Americans.

Reunification and Entrance to the World Stage

With one struggle over, another was beginning. The victors to the North now had to undertake the marathon process of stitching together two halves of a fractured nation. The imposition of socialism on their capitalist brothers to the South would require a significant political crackdown. While there were no mass executions of South Vietnamese (a consequence of defeat that many had feared), there was still a punishment to be dealt out.

Over the next 10 years, more than a million Southerners — businessmen, journalists, politicians, along with American collaborators and supporters of the Southern regime — were herded into "re-education camps", with "education" being an Orwellian euphemism. Those imprisoned were forced to live and do hard labour in appalling conditions. Fear of re-education, persecution and relocation sparked a refugee crisis in the South. Close to two million "boat people" took to sea, fleeing their socialist paradise for any other nation they could sail to.

This modern era of Vietnam began as one of isolationism, though they did attack Cambodia, in retaliation for Khmer raids on Vietnamese towns and villages along their shared border. They won that fight, as seems to be tradition for the Vietnamese military. Hanoi knocked out the Cambodian government in Phnom Penh and swapped in a pro-Viet regime. It wasn't long after this that they neutered (another) Chinese attack from the North. When it came to guns, Vietnam just couldn't lose.

If only their economy could have enjoyed the same level of success. Vietnam's economic development was stunted as it hit a few of the same roadblocks Communist China had before them. Collectivism and the top-down pressure of state control had a ruinous effect on the economy. Poverty was as rampant as ever and Vietnam had to go on financial life support, which came in the form of a few billion dollars in annual aid doled out by Russia.

Soon after the death of postwar Communist leader Le Duan in 1986, Vietnam followed their Soviet Big Brother's lead by easing the iron grip it held on its own market. The nation remained fiercely and proudly Communist (in the political sense) but by the early 1990s, legislation had been passed that allowed private businesses to start making a comeback.

Vietnam Today

Fast-forward a couple decades and you'll find a Vietnam that has emerged from the turbulence that defined it for so long. The country currently holds a population of 91 million and the conditions now exist to allow for a growing middle class.

Vietnam is still developing, still grapples with poverty, and still has a long way to go. But household income has been skyrocketing since the year 2000, the economy is growing at 6–7 per cent annually, and Vietnam is now a member of the World Trade Organization.

The US lifted its 30-year economic embargo on its former enemy in 1994, and in 2016 President Obama visited Hanoi and announced the end of an arms embargo as well. This was mainly a geopolitical flex calculated to rattle a surging Beijing, but such a deal wouldn't have been possible if diplomatic relations hadn't been restored between America and Vietnam. Obama's visit made him the third consecutive US President to visit Hanoi, after George W. Bush and Bill Clinton.

Foreign businesses are setting up branches on Vietnamese soil in greater numbers, and at the same more and more expats and backpackers are flying over here (about seven million in 2015, up from roughly two million in the year 2000) to congregate in the cafés and clubs of Hanoi and Saigon.

And this is probably where you enter the story.

CHAPTER 3

PEOPLE

**The only normal people are the ones
you don't know very well.**

— Alfred Adler, philosopher and psychiatrist

Representations of the Vietnamese in Western media tend to be from "the" war, whether in newsreel footage or clips from the movie *Apocalypse Now*. The Vietnamese shown there were either gun-toting aggressors or villagers stuck in the middle of the fight.

But we're now decades removed from that era and its dark circumstances, and those images are no longer relevant. So who are they now, these people whose neighbourhood you're about to move into?

Well, at the risk of being trite, I'll say that they're just like you.

Expats to have one of two reactions after arriving in Vietnam: Some of them will assimilate, make local friends quickly and forever gush about Vietnamese hospitality. And there are others who get ripped off by a cab driver and then forever deride the place as a lawless wasteland.

What is Vietnam? Is it welcoming or abrasive? It's both. You will meet incredibly warm, open people. And you're also going to get scammed, at least for a buck or five. Those are both givens.

The Vietnamese are propelled by the same motivations as you are. They struggle with bosses and traffic and traffic (not a typo—it deserves to be mentioned twice), and keeping all the plates spinning. They want the best for their families and they want to enjoy their lives. A country's political and economic circumstances are the box in which the population is poured, and the people react accordingly. Everyone is doing the best they can. When I run into some frustrating quirk of Viet culture, I try to re-remember that I'd be acting no differently were I born here.

Being a primarily homogeneous nation, 85 per cent of the Vietnam's population hails from the Viet (also called "Kinh") ethnic group. Taking up smaller slices of the pie chart are the Tay, Khmer, Thai, Muong, Nung and Hoa groups. Ethnic minorities generally do not reside in the major cities, and instead maintain a traditional lifestyle in the hills and lowlands.

VIETNAMESE VALUES
Family First

Unless they're off studying at university, you can find a majority of young Vietnamese living with their families. This is not because they think Mom and Dad are amazing roommates, it's because that's how it's done here.

If you're a 24-year-old Vietnamese guy who's been living under what seems like a parental dictatorship for 24 years, when do you finally get your own place? Usually, when you get married. And sometimes not — with economic conditions being as they are, some newlyweds continue to live with one of their families for a spell after the wedding.

Generally, familial devotion and familial proximity go hand in hand.

There are always escape routes, though, for those who crave their independence and autonomy. Some of my single Vietnamese friends have found a loophole to the default housing situation: They move away from their hometowns and attend university in the big city. After graduation, they sprint straight into the workplace, a move that necessitates urban accommodation.

Mom and Dad will miss you — but how can they summon you home if you're out there making them proud?

It's a little different in the South (which is almost like a different country, the more you get to know the people there). In Saigon, you'll talk to more young, single people who live on their own.

If you don't live in the same city or town as your family, you might be expected to make a homecoming pilgrimage at least once every few weeks, but only if the journey is feasible — I can't imagine Vietnamese parents demanding you take a flight from Saigon back to Hanoi every other Saturday.

Face

Being aware of the sociological concept of "face" is going to help you out as you stride through the minefield of Vietnamese culture. This will become especially true in the halls of business, if that's what you're here for.

Face is social currency, and it can be given (or lost) at the personal, team, corporate or national level. Vietnamese people conduct their interactions in order to give each other face, keep others from losing it and to preserve their own.

Simply put, face refers to the possession of dignity, honour and respect in the eyes of others. This is why guilty parties will be highly reluctant to own up to wrongdoing, as that will cause them to lose the face that they've built up. That's why, if possible, blame will go unassigned. Being that we live in an imperfect world where errors are common and sins are many, you can start to imagine the delicate diplomacy that saving face requires.

The more I learn about face, the more I come to view it as stubborn ego-preservation by way of habitually adjusting the truth. Not my thing — but it is theirs.

The Commandments of "Face"

You're a smart cookie, so some of these will be pretty intuitive. But since I did all this research, here they are anyway:

- Causing someone embarrassment by pointing out a mistake they've made (even if it's a blatant, damaging mistake) will make them lose face. The same goes for proving someone wrong, or pointing out deception.
- Rejecting an invitation from someone will cause them lose face, too. Overt, pointed criticism of someone, or their actions, will have the same effect.
- If you turn down someone's offer to pay for coffee or a meal, they will lose face.
- Arguing and shouting in public will result in a net loss of face in both parties, at least in the eyes of bystanders.
- Paying someone a compliment will give them face. The more sincere and personalized, the better.
- Take your time with small talk — showing interest in other gives them face. Building up each other's face (establishing polite rapport) is a key initial step in a business relationship.

Basically? Be charming, and try not to embarrass anyone.

The Prize of Reputation

Here's the life script you're handed as a Vietnamese kid. Don't worry about memorizing it, as there aren't that many beats:

- Earn the grades to gain admission to a reputable school, and do well there.
- Secure a good job after graduation, and do well there. Sound familiar?

You'll obviously find these stage directions mirrored in the West — but you'll also find more rebels there, too, proudly marching down their individual paths. If they go broke or fail spectacularly, it's usually seen as being on them, not their family.

In Vietnam there's a cultural premium placed on the family name, and keeping it clean and unblemished as a battle standard. It's important to honour your parents by succeeding for them—and for their parents too. You've got to keep the streak going; families derive pride from owning a long, multi-generational chain of success in school and at work. Vietnamese youth have an entire family tree to consider as they plot out their next moves.

And if you, the diligent youngster, happen to forget these considerations—expect to be reminded in short order.

Some Vietnamese find themselves studying at university even if they truly don't see the benefit of it. I spoke to a treelancer who felt that her college education had been an unnecessary detour. Then why'd she go?

"We go to university for our parents, not for us."

On the bright side, paying for school won't nuke your financial future, like it can in the West. Tuition at a public university runs about US$200 a year here. In contrast, I think I paid about US$200 a minute for my BA from an American school.

Status

"Status" is another social currency in Vietnam, and deference to those who have it is expected here. How do you earn status? Well, the easiest way is also the slowest. All you have to do is get older. Being educated is a status boost as well—but we're talking highly educated. Mere college attendance is no longer what it once was. The Vietnamese job market is now reaching a saturation point where a BA no longer has the heft it used to. To keep up in the educational arms race, more Vietnamese are taking the postgrad route—just like all of us back in the West.

In days gone by, you really couldn't buy your way into status. But the rulebook is different now. Financial success has come to be as revered, respected and resented in the same proportions you'll see in capitalist nations.

"Money matters now," a friend says. Free enterprise has arrived in Vietnam, a country that was holding fast to hardcore Communist ideals just a few decades ago. Another friend (a Saigoner) takes it further, saying, "Today, rich is cool."

When you meet people of a higher status, show respect with a slow nod or short bow. In social situations, such as a meal at someone's home, greet the person of highest status first. If it's not apparent who that is, then greet the elders before anyone else.

Upward Mobility

Now that the hurdles of war and colonization have been cleared for a generation, Vietnam continues its run into the future. As the country works its way up the scale, its people rise with it. Per capita GDP has increased an average of 6.4% a year since the new millennium started. People do have to work hard. But fewer and fewer of them are mired in poverty.

Businessmen and women now own the moneyed persona, and the fine handbags and killer watches that come with it, as symbols of legitimacy that will help with prospective deals and connections.

There's another reason to show off, and it's a relatable one. It's "I worked my hands to the bone for this, you better believe I'm going to enjoy it."

They've brought status to their family name, not through age or education, but through business. Those with money are no longer perceived as sellouts or empty suits.

That is, as long as they're not obnoxious about it. Like anywhere else, you have your elite. They pack the Starbucks, they flash iPad Pros and diamond cufflinks, and their Ferraris snort in frustration while idling in gridlock.

But not all of those whom fortune has smiled upon flash their excess. Why?

Well, fortune hasn't yet smiled on a great many people who live here. And the lucky ones don't want to get robbed.

Age (Way, Way, Way) Before Beauty

Status is king, and over the course of my cultural investigation I've observed that the older folks really do enjoy it. I'd also be unsurprised if any scientific data emerged illustrating any reality-distorting superiority complex among them.

One of my adult students, a woman in her 30s, once asked me to explain a concept, and we ended up needing a Vietnamese translation for one of the words. My teacher's assistant, who was a 19 year-old college student, came over to help out—but my student shooed her away. My TA had the answer, but my student deemed it unacceptable for the TA, a younger woman, to provide it. My student looked it up on her phone instead.

Granny on the Loose

Then there was the time I was on my motorbike and was railroaded by a Vietnamese woman driving out of a blind alley I was passing. (Pro-tip: Honk your horn at intersections. If you're not going to be seen, make sure you're heard).

When the woman hit me, it felt like taking a low tackle. We both wobbled and skidded as we flirted with disaster, but I managed to brake and plant my feet on the ground so I wouldn't tip over. She stayed upright, too. (Probably because she's used to collisions, I thought.)

Her tire had made contact with my ankle, and I checked for blood (just a trickle) and then processed what had just happened — and found myself at a loss. She hadn't slowed, looked, or honked as she reached the road. She'd just gone for it. There was no way to break down the situation other than this: she was driving recklessly. And if she hit someone, well, that was their problem.

I spread my hands, as one does, trying to invite an apologetic look or some other sort of contrition from her.

Her reaction?

She screamed and jabbed a finger into my chest a few times. In her reality, the crash was my fault.

Good to know, for future games of motorbike chicken.

"Older people can be curmudgeons," a co-worker told me. "In those situations it's best to take the blame, say you're sorry, and move on."

I had a flashback to the moment of impact.

"Yes, if you're able to move on," I said.

VIETNAMESE MEN

In a perfect world, a Vietnamese man will achieve financial stability before he marries.

When it comes to families, we're encountering some classic traditionalism. Vietnamese men grow up wearing the mantle of familial devotion, and when they start their own, the goal is to lead and provide.

Those tasks are expected from him. What he hopes to receive from his wife and children is respect for the money he brings home, and for the effort it took to earn. He expects his wife to keep the home running smoothly, so that it's a sanctuary where he can recover from his labours.

But men who are unable to find work find themselves frustrated that they've failed to provide for his family the way they are expected to. Many while away the hour at home and find themselves with little better to do than unscrew a bottle of *ruou de* (rice wine).

A friend of mine works for an NGO that focuses on the economically disadvantaged, and tells me that it's in these poorer communities where domestic abuse can be rampant.

VIETNAMESE WOMEN

The role of a woman in the Vietnamese family (and in most families world-over) is to keep the show running. They're the producers and support structures for their husbands and kids.

Besides that, they still have to work. Vietnamese men may toil to provide, but their wives can match them.

"There are housewives in Vietnam, but not too many," one of my co-workers told me. "Obviously, if you have two incomes, that's much better."

When a household needs a second revenue stream,

A Vietnamese woman prepares the day's goods for sale at the market.

A Vietnamese woman selling her wares on the street.

Vietnamese women answer the call. Walk for a few blocks in any town or city and you'd notice that nearly every restaurant and shop is staffed by women, grinding away the hours on the clock before they head home and run through a list of domestic chores. Many women cobble together a low salary every month—the average hovers, stubbornly, somewhere between US$140 and US$160. But it's necessary; the financial cost of raising a child leaves many women with no other option but to rise early and hustle deep into the evening.

How do women view their workload?

"We like to work to build our own careers, and make our own money," said one friend.

"Being powerful in the background is appealing," said another. "We know the man wants to be the 'king'. But we like being the queen behind the king." For context, it's worth remembering that Vietnamese women usually don't take their husband's family names when they get married. They retain that one identity marker, no matter where life takes them.

COURTSHIP AND DATING

Couples begin to form at the expected time — somewhere in the middle of secondary school, Vietnamese Romeos will begin to hint at their intentions. My friends tell me that even if the girl likes the boy in return, she'll hold back, expecting to be pursued. And maybe, just maybe, she's hoping to inspire definitive overtures from the young lad?

"Based on movies, we think that European men are very romantic with their girlfriends," a friend tells me. "Many Vietnamese boys are not really this way."

Dates are simple affairs. The young couple will see a movie or go out to eat. From the outside, it seems that an extra hour would have to be added to the standard day in order to make time for dates: They must fit, somehow, into the mystical, seldom-present time slot that exists somewhere after studies have been concluded, but before the drop-dead hour of youngsters' curfew. But the better the parents know their daughter's suitor, and the higher their regard for him, the more latitude the young couple is given. (Ingratiating yourself with your significant other's family seems to be a non-negotiable part of the deal.) Vietnamese culture still leans

---

Families and Divorce

A Vietnamese friend of mine is 25 and single, and her mother just got divorced. This once-unfathomable process is now seen as on option as Vietnam continues to thaw out of its rigid traditionalism. The mother apparently wrestled with the choice to end her marriage, and decided it would be best to do so after her children had grown and left the nest.

"Husbands don't matter," my friend's mother told her. "Having a child matters."

Another friend of mine told me his sister is having marital trouble. Will she split from her husband?

"No, not until the children have grown," he told me. "Her first duty is keeping the family strong."

conservative, and as such you won't see much PDA among couples on the streets.

And if you thought your last blind date was awkward, over here it's still common for parents to conspire to set their son or daughter up with a pre-selected companion, perhaps the child of friends. The Vietnamese choose who they like to marry, but never discount the sway a spirited campaign of parental lobbying may have.

GAY AND LESBIAN SCENE

Displaying affection on the streets is taboo (a statement that holds more true in the north of the country than the south), but you might catch a peck here or a lap-sit there, especially if the lovebirds in question are students.

But one thing I don't think you'll see for a little while is a same-sex couple holding hands.

Where does Vietnam stand on LGBT rights? Can we say, the social equivalent of the American 1960s? Considering Vietnam's deeply conservative traditions, that's a fair assumption.

But the cause has actually been slowly progressing. Vietnam's first gay pride parade was organized in 2012. As of 2015, gay marriage is no longer banned. This legislative shift has quietly signalled that homosexuality is no longer viewed by the government as a "social evil" on the level of prostitution or the use of hard drugs. Gay weddings are now permitted—though they're not yet fully recognized by the state (think American civil unions). And as of 2017, it became legally permissible for the Vietnamese to change their gender.

One explanation for the country's evolution on this issue can be found in its government. Lawmakers stand at the helm of a de facto atheist state, and so they're unhampered by the theological considerations their Western counterparts face.

Gay progress is instead just (just!) a question of how quickly the movement can gain favour in a country with a deep patriarchal tradition. All recent progress aside, this will still be like asking a container ship to turn on a dime. Whatever the younger Vietnamese sentiment is, they still have yesterday's generation (their parents) to appease. A heterosexual marriage followed by the growth of a nuclear family is still as culturally revered as you'd expect. Many Vietnamese gays lead double lives—participating in a family-sanctioned marriage in public while carrying on same-sex relations in secret.

Both of the major cities have small gay scenes. There are more nightlife options in Saigon, it being the bigger city. If you're visiting for a short time, it's good to know that gay tour companies (Gay Hanoi Tours, Rainbow Tourism Vietnam, etc.) operate freely within the country.

Despite the parades and the new laws, current estimates on Vietnam's gay population are that around a third are still closeted. And—this doesn't happen to everyone, but—a percentage of young gays report having been beaten by their classmates or parents for being out. This is more frequent in the North, which leans more conservative.

One of my co-workers, a Hanoian, is a young gay man who's had a boyfriend for some time now. Has he ever told his parents?

"Absolutely not. When my family asks me when I'm going to get a girlfriend, I deflect the question and say I'm focusing on work right now." He feels there's still a "terrible" homophobic discrimination lingering in Vietnam.

RELIGION

While there's something of a minor personality cult centred around Uncle Ho, it's nothing like what you'll find in North Korea, and you wouldn't call it a religion.

Nor does Vietnam have anything in common with other Communist nations who have employed religious persecution. An article in Vietnam's 1992 Constitution guaranteed freedom of religious practice by stating "all religions are equal before the law." So, no matter what you box you check when it comes to worship, you should be all right over here.

Most Vietnamese do not profess allegiance to any faith. As of 2014, more than 73 per cent of the population identified as atheist or non-religious. But the misleading thing about this 73 per cent is that many of the same people who don't report themselves as religious also follow the traditions of something called Tam Giao, or the "triple religion". Tam Giao is best explained as a loose, informal hybrid of Buddhist, Confucian and Taoist tenets.

A three-headed super-religion? How do you even begin to subscribe to such a thing? Are there three times as many rules?

To keep it simple, just remember that Vietnamese customs include honouring ancestors on the anniversaries of their deaths. On these days, a Vietnamese family will ring a bell, burn some incense, and pray for the spirits of the dead.

Ancestor worship and its customs pervade daily Vietnamese life to an extent that they are not even thought of as a religious practice. It's sort of a vague given, like the notion of America being generally a "Christian" nation, which sees people from all walks of life packing church pews on Easter Sunday. Most restaurants, offices, and small businesses have a small Buddhist shrine on display,

A man offers prayers at a Buddhist temple in Hanoi.

and nearly every home does as well.

It's said that during the Day of Wandering Souls (during the seventh month of the lunar calendar), spirits are briefly freed from the afterlife and can come back to their homes. Of course, if your home's been torn down and the plot colonized by a shopping mall, then you have nowhere to go — so Vietnamese families will pray for lost spirits as well.

Astrological superstitions have lost ground in the modern age, but that doesn't mean they're gone. It's still common to check in with a fortune teller before making important decisions or scheduling a wedding. And about half of the young adults I work with have said that they espouse the supernatural. They'll say that they've never seen a ghost, but that doesn't keep them from thinking they one day might.

That's a look into the traditionalist population. The remainder of Vietnam's devout are generally split among six other religions. Besides certain percentages of Catholics,

Protestants and Muslims, there're about two million followers of Cao Dai, or Caodaism, a monotheistic indigenous religion that arose in the 1920s, and also 1.2 million devotees of Hoa Hao Buddhism. Hoa Hao is a pared-down offshoot of "regular" Buddhism, and focuses more on home prayer and interaction with the needy than on temple worship and divine rituals.

But since there are more than 10 million Buddhists in Vietnam, you'll get a lot of good photos for your album when you walk past any of the country's hundreds of Buddhist pagodas.

Buddhist temples complexes generally feature a tiered tower (pagoda) placed in a gated courtyard. Since most temples have a pagoda, the words "pagoda" and "temple" are often used interchangeably when referring to places of worship.

Some European Catholic influence remains spliced into the DNA of Vietnam — remember that South Vietnamese president Ngo Dinh Diem followed the faith (and felt compelled to persecute Buddhists as a result). Visible evidence of Catholicism in Vietnam includes the Notre-Dame Cathedral Basilica of Saigon. And up in Hanoi, near Hoan Kiem Lake, is St Joseph's Cathedral. It's open for mass on Sundays, though you'll have to be fluent in Vietnamese if you want to get anything out of the sermon.

CHAPTER 4

SOCIALIZING AND FITTING IN

❝Travellers never think they are the foreigners.**❞**

— Mason Cooley, writer

A TALE OF TWO CITIES

I'd heard stories of animosity between Northerners and Southerners, and was curious about how much of this was fuelled by the legacy of the war. I was also wondering how there was any way it couldn't be so. After all, there are still many people alive who remember the bullets fired as brother fought brother.

My unscientific sample of sentiment, conducted over a few dozen rounds of coffee in both Hanoi and Saigon, gave me some insights. Sure, you'll find some exceptions, but here are some defensible generalizations:

- Northerners (who were victorious, remember) are more likely to explain any spats or digs as brotherly. They say that any regional friction can be marked down to the sheer distance between the top and the bottom of such a long country, and to the cultural variations that 1,600km allow. (I'm from the American East Coast, so the comparative analogy I first reached for was New York vs. Boston.) But Saigon hosts a people who were beaten. It's a place that has been passed between powers and reset a few times, and people will actually say things like, "The French and the Americans built some amazing things here—and the Communists got rid of them."
- Southerners (Saigoners, specifically) are big-city slickers and they'll generally give it to you straight, even if it comes off as rude. Because Northerners are

more mindful of preserving face, they'll tip-toe up the pathway, picking their words carefully so they don't offend you.

- Northerners are more frugal and save money for landmark purchases (property or a home), and for their family's future. Southerners do that too, but find excuses to be looser with their wallets. They're not afraid of generosity and treating friends and relatives to a nice night out.
- Both like to mock the other's accent.
- Hanoi is traditional to a fault, as its bonds to the nation's founding are immeasurably stronger. Though foreign corporations maintain a (limited) presence there—which is all but unavoidable in the globalized era, Hanoi still remains as Vietnamese as it's possible to be. And Southerners see the capital city the way I do: more restrained and worn-down than Saigon. Meanwhile, take a hike through Saigon and see a city of taboos: Tattoos, flamboyant lifestyles (with hairstyles to match), short skirts and a clutch of

barely-disguised, ahem, well let's just refer to them as "houses of ill-repute". Go downtown, and you'll see so many McDonald's and Burger Kings that you might wonder if there's any Vietnamese food to be had. It makes sense, since Saigon has been mainlining foreign influence ever since it was a port city developed and administered by the French. (Saigon has only existed for one-fifth as long as Hanoi has.) Northerners see it as a past and present sellout, an imitation of Bangkok and perhaps a betrayal of the Viet spirit that a formal name change did little to stop.

- To be sure, you'll find legions of patriots in the South. But others are unmoved by the new 7.2m-tall statue of Uncle Ho standing over a grand promenade, in front of the golden City Hall that bears his name. They still commonly reject the labelling of the conquering Communist elite, and continue to refer to their city as Saigon. But they've accepted how the story ends, with the North's ultimate victory. As a friend of mine in Saigon said, "We're different. But we respect each

The new statue of Uncle Ho standing in front of Saigon City Hall.

other. And we're tired of protesting and fighting; we don't want to do that forever."

WHAT ABOUT EVERYONE ELSE?

City folk regard their rural brethren as honest, curious, salt-of-the-earth types. No real surprises there.

Based on my travels, I'd agree with this. However, people in the country don't really speak English, so their hospitality has its limits. Unless you've started hacking away at the odyssey that is learning Vietnamese, it'll hard for you to do much but smile at each other.

"It's like every country," my Vietnamese friends say. "People are cooler in the cities, and warmer in the countryside."

Others will say things such as, "In the countryside, they're narrow-minded and they live in the past."

Sounds familiar — I've heard the same exact thing in New Hampshire, when people make blanket statements about Alabama and its neighbours (without ever having been there).

Yours truly, having a seafood meal with some students. Dinner selfies are both ubiquitous and mandatory here, too.

Stranger Things

No matter where you are in the country, there are a few oddities you should be forewarned about.

- **Mole Hair**: Apparently, it's considered lucky to let hair grow out of a mole… forever. It's rare, but you'll see what looks to be a literal ponytail sprouting out of a man's face or neck, sometimes dangling as far as halfway down his torso. Best to avert your gaze during mealtime.

- **Sneezing and Coughing**: The Vietnamese won't cover their faces before blasting the room with a sneeze. They'll also look at you quite blankly if you respond to said sneeze with a "bless you".

- **Spitting**: It's acceptable for smokers to hock up a nice gob of phlegm and shoot it out, letting it fly free and splat wherever it may. This habit is dying out as the new century wears on, though.

- **Pinky Nails**: Some men will fastidiously trim their fingernails… well, nine of them. They might let the pinky nail on either hand grow out a few centimetres (a "few" is an understatement — it looks like Wolverine forgot to complete his manicure). Some explanations include:
  - It's a play at showing status, by advertising that they're not the type of stiff who must commit himself to manual labour to make a living.
  - As folklore tells it, rich or fortunate people are apparently born with a pinky finger that reaches the last knuckle of the ring finger, and so by growing out this last pinky nail, some men are bridging the digit gap and willing themselves to riches.
  - It makes picking their noses easier.

Now you've been warned, so you won't be completely perplexed when you feel a scrape on the inside of your wrist while shaking hands with a Vietnamese man.

HOW THEY SEE YOU

Urban Vietnamese are used to foreigners. (Which is to be expected. I mean, we've been puttering around here for centuries). They'll generally leave you alone and let you carry on as you were, but they also come up to your table at the *bia hoi* (beer garden) and begin interviewing you.

To them, you're the closest thing to a crash-landed alien, which naturally provokes curiosity. (Or maybe the interest is mostly a front and they want to practice their English, but let's give them the benefit of the doubt.)

Every place has its angels, its regular folk, and its bad eggs. All over Vietnam, the people I've met have been amiable and agreeable enough. I've only been snapped at a few times (usually in motorbike-related incidents).

In the tourist zones of Saigon, the locals won't even acknowledge your existence if there's no sale to be made. Several friends of mine who visited the city report being flatly ignored when asking for help or directions. You can think of this as rude, or perhaps just efficient; it's a hard-knock life for much of the populace, and they've learned to only focus on what'll put food on the table.

Then there's unsolicited help, which is rarely given for free. A Vietnamese woman approached my friends and offered to help them find their hostel. After she guided them to it, she asked for money, and wouldn't leave the lobby until they gave her 20,000 VND. Such is the nature of the beast in Vietnam—you could be carrying on a seemingly casual

---

Financial Perspectives

I was on my home from work once and picked up a jug of water from my corner store. While I was paying, the shopkeeper got a glimpse of my weekly salary in cash, which happened to be peeking out of my pocket.

He said, "Wow, you are very rich!"

I almost corrected him, but realized it would be relatively insulting to do so. From his perspective, I was rich.

And the locals are aware of it. Economic wants have given rise to scammers. "A lot of the general public can't communicate with you," a Vietnamese friend told me. "But it's in their interest to learn how, because they see you as a mobile ATM."

This friend said that he was once having dinner with a group of Americans, and when the bill came, the Americans were charged an extra 10,000 VND for the same meal that he'd also ordered.

They didn't notice, but he did. He asked the server about it, and the explanation he received was, "It's because they eat more than you do."

---

interaction with someone, only to find out later that it had been a business transaction the entire time.

The Elephant in the Room

As an American, there was a mite of concern in the back of mind upon my arrival, since the US maintained a, let's say vigorous, presence in the country just 40 years ago. For perspective, let's flip it around: Can you imagine how Americans would treat citizens of a country who'd deployed combat troops on their home coil, 40 years ago?

But when I tell the Vietnamese where I'm from, there's no friction, no awkwardness, no hesitation. The conversation just keeps going. They did win that war, after all, and victory can be a soothing thing. At this point, nationalistic outrage would be something like the Americans still holding a grudge against Germany.

The nation is now united and proudly independent, and memories of war move further into the background each day.

My Vietnamese friends have mentioned that it's in the

countryside where yesterday's resentment can still hold strong. More specifically, members of the rural elderly population retain a distrust of foreigners, and reportedly view them as "liars" or "untrustworthy".

One young man I talked to said, "We know the history, but that happened before. You," he gestured to me, "didn't do anything to us."

Racism

You can of course flip through the Vietnamese historical record and highlight a clutch of examples of discrimination

---

Parking Enforcement

There's only one ime I've been on the receiving edge of blunt, Grade-A, no-doubt-about-it racism in Vietnam.

I was with a friend and scouting for a parking spot in Hanoi's Night Market. The locals monetize the sidewalks for parking during high-capacity events and they make a comparative killing, charging 10,000–20,000 VND per bike over the course of the night. There was a stretch of sidewalk open and I pushed my scooter up over the curb and slid off my helmet. That's when the man in charge of the street stepped over and waved me away. I fired up my bike again and moved back into the street, thinking there was something I didn't know — maybe that spot was reserved, something like that.

I looked for my friend, but he wasn't with me; he'd already parked his bike and gotten off.

"Wait, why not me?" I asked the Vietnamese man. I pulled 20,000 VND out of my pocket and offered it to the Vietnamese man, who ignored it and gave a weird little chuckle before again waving me away.

That's when I put together what was happening. I wasn't allowed to park there because I'm white. My friend? He's Indonesian — and presumably the local mistook him for one of his own.

I drove away before my temper spiked.

What does this say about the Vietnamese? Not much, really. This guy I encountered was an outlier — only he knows exactly what his deal was. And I've been allowed to park a thousand other times in a thousand other places by a thousand other locals.

---

and racism. And similarly, prejudices still exist.

I asked some friends about who the prejudices were directed towards, and China was mentioned a few times. The two neighbours have a lengthy, intertwined history that's sometimes exploded into violence. Current animosities may be rooted in disputes over resource-rich swaths of the South China Sea.

When foreigners marry Vietnamese, it's safe to say that the Vietnamese parents aren't swinging from the rafters when they hear the news. A Vietnamese friend of mine has dated a few foreign men over the past few years. I asked her if she'd introduced any of these boyfriends to her parents. She laughed and said, "Absolutely not. Never."

Homogeneity is implicitly prized. Look back to the post-war period and you'll find half-Vietnamese, half-American "war children" having a rough go of it here.

MILESTONES AND CELEBRATIONS
Birthdays

The average birthday celebration is small, simple recognizable affair. There's a meal and cake, along with a few gifts from friends and family. That may not be very surprising, I know, but the following might be:

In the countryside, where incomes are lower, a birthday party will probably be a luxury. That, or the very celebration of one's birthday, might be a foreign idea, something that has yet to be absorbed into the fabric of traditional society. A friend of mine, who moved to Hanoi from an outlying village, told me that her father doesn't know when her birthday is. He knows the calendar year, but can't get any more specific than that when pressed.

Engagement Traditions

Take the shyness endemic to adolescent dating and extrapolate it out to an engagement, and you'll correctly figure that ostentatious public proposals (with marching bands and the like) are a rarity. Most couples will get engaged privately, and the proposal is a simple formality that cements the pre-marital discussions that have already taken place — discussions that were guided and influenced by frequent input from both sets of parents.

Many Vietnamese couples go from betrothal to wedding in about three months — a speed that would give American wedding planners anxiety attacks.

Vietnamese engagements have taken Western overtones in the postwar period. This starts with the engagement ring; as it was a foreign idea, Vietnamese women were never presented with one. But those of my students in their twenties

A couple's engagement photo shoot at Hoan Kiem Lake. The bride-to-be is wearing the traditional *ao dai.*

tell me that one is expected these days. The young men in the class groaned—they have to factor in a new expense, one their fathers didn't have to deal with, into the courtship process.

On any given day in downtown Hanoi, there will be engaged couples posing for their wedding photos in front of the Louis Vutton store in black suits and white or gold gowns.

If the couple-to-be see you as a close friend, they'll ask you to join them at their betrothal ceremony (*an hoi*). The *an hoi* is also referred to as a *le dinh hon*, or engagement party.

Similar to Western rehearsal dinners, the *an hoi* will occur a day or two before the wedding (placing the ceremony in the same time frame as the nuptials prevents family members from far-flung provinces from having to make two trips in service of the same wedding). The ceremony is held at the bride's home. If you're invited, dress formally and bring a cash gift (for appropriate amounts, see page 64).

After the introductions, the groom's family may present a few gifts, and then the two families have a small meal and drink tea together. Following this, a representative from the groom's family (typically a grandfather, uncle or some other de facto patriarch) will stand and formally ask the bride's parents for their daughter's hand in marriage.

To me, this exchange registers as a bit dated. I asked a local friend of mine who will be getting hitched next year if these traditions are still adhered to in 2017.

"Of course," she said.

Today's youth are right now in the middle of transcending long-held superstitions, but tradition is still king, and it's the traditional parents who are calling the shots.

The Big Day

On the wedding day, gifts wrapped in red paper are presented to the couple. Then there's the ring exchange and prayers in front of the bride's family altar (another semi-private ceremony, just for members of the wedding party). Once that's over, the bride and groom head to the reception to meet guests and consume a six-to-10 course feast. If you weren't invited to the ceremony itself, this is where you'll first see the newlyweds.

A Vietnamese couple takes their vows in a church.

Be punctual! Treat the reception as you would a flight. The wedding date (as well as the schedule of events) is chosen after consulting with a fortune teller.

Perhaps with the aim of balancing out the festive responsibilities of hosting the *an hoi*, the groom's family is generally charged with the reception. If the wedding is held in the city then the reception will likely be at a hotel. Families with disposable income will probably show off a little bit by picking a luxurious venue. Other families, lacking such means, might hold the reception at the groom's home.

A Vietnamese wedding procession on its way to the reception.

Pro-tip: If you have time to chase some down, it couldn't hurt to bring a small bouquet of white or yellow flowers for the bride.

If you're lucky enough to know the right people, you could be in for a wild night. A friend of mine was invited to a reception that eventually transmuted in a giant rave, with smoke machines and two emcees rapping on stage during a laser light show.

Honeymoons aren't yet a common fixture in the Vietnamese wedding timeline. What happens instead is that after the wedding ceremony, most newlyweds instead stage an anticlimactic return to their

When attending a wedding, it's impossible to be overdressed. "Wear the most formal outfit you possibly can," a friend told me. "But women shouldn't wear white, that colour is for the bride."

Money as a Wedding Gift

Don't stress about picking the perfect gift for the happy couple — cash is all you need to bring. There are no written rules for how much to give, but there are some unwritten rules, which I've decided to rebelliously describe here:

- If you're attending the ceremony solo, bring 100,000–300,000 VND (US$5–15).
- If you're there with your family, anywhere from 500,000–1,000,000 VND (approximately US$23–46) should do.
- And if you're especially close to the bride or groom, it doesn't hurt to go even higher than that, if you can swing it.

There should be a heart-shaped box set out at the wedding reception; that's where you should drop your envelope. If you know the bride or groom particularly well, you could also hand the envelope to their parents.

And after that? It's time to fill up on food and Tiger beer.

family homes and stay there for three or four days. Why? They're waiting for the most auspicious day to move in to their new home together. Like the wedding date, the move-in date is also selected under the guidance of a fortune teller.

Funerals

One day you will wake up to sombre, off-key Vietnamese folk music wailing from somewhere in your neighbourhood. It's almost certain that this disruption will be a funeral.

The end of life is as much of a community affair as it is in the West. In the case that I witnessed, a local *bia hoi* was taken over for mourning purposes. For two days, the road was all but blocked off by a white tent. Inside were rows of plastic chairs arrayed around a shrine, bouquets of flowers the size of asteroids, and an oversized portrait of the deceased. The speakers never stopped blaring their forlorn soundtrack, which had the subliminal effect of depressing the whole block for a few days.

That's the public-facing side of it. If you're invited to a funeral at someone's home, you'll probably find the casket placed in the middle of the home's living area. Guests will move past it to burn incense and offer prayers for the soul of the departed. It's not essential to wear black (that colour is no longer reserved for mourning purposes). But just keep in mind that if you're invited to a funeral, you shouldn't wear any bright colours.

There's some symmetry between weddings and funerals, in that you bring money to a funeral as well to help the family through their hardship. How much, exactly? Follow the same price scale as you do for a wedding. In the family's home, burning incense will be set on a table; that's where you'll place the envelope (unlike for weddings, the colour of the envelope does not matter). Alternatively, you might hand it to the deceased's family. Just do what everyone else does, and you'll be fine. A large meal of chicken and sticky rice is eaten at some point during the proceedings.

VISITING SOMEONE'S HOME

So, you've been invited to your coworker's house for dinner. Don't worry about this (I'm sure you can find something else to worry about in Vietnam, anyway), because when you're a guest, less is more.

The first time you visit someone's home, all you really need to do is show up, hang out and eat. If they've invited you over, you're going to be a guest, and they want to give you the full extent of their hospitality.

My friends have told me that it could be seen as a slight if a guest brings food with them. That implies either the guest thinks the host can't afford to feed another mouth, or that he doesn't much confidence in the host's culinary prowess.

One exception: You can bring some bread or fruit over, if you're keen on making a good showing. Some apples,

bananas or oranges are fine. These offerings are acceptable because they won't be seen as a "challenge" to the evening meal.

Liquor is another matter entirely. A bottle of whiskey (of neither cheap nor extravagant price) is the de facto gift for the man of the house.

Bringing your host some flowers is a nice touch, but it's not mandatory. Pick up a bouquet of anything you think is pretty—orchids, daisies, lilies—anything except roses. The Vietnamese reserve roses as gifts for lovers.

Take your shoes off at the door before you enter the home. In Vietnam, it is not typical to wear shoes inside the house.

The Meal

I imagined Vietnamese families all sat on the floor when they ate, but regular old dining room tables are more common than I thought. All the dishes comprising the meal will probably already be spread out on the table when it's time to take a seat. In all likelihood, your hosts will show you where to sit. Seating arrangements have a lot to do with age and status. In any event, it can't hurt to respect the oldest person at the table by waiting for them to start eating before you do.

Then you're off to the races. Help yourself to the food, while constantly doing mental tabulation to make it seem like you're not eating too much (don't be greedy) or too little (what, you don't like it?) of any one dish.

It's a gesture of goodwill to pick up food and place it in someone else's bowl for them. (Use the utensils provided, not your personal chopsticks, you heathen!) And it seems that diners must take the contradictory stance of profusely complimenting the host's cooking, while avoiding being "gluttony" by taking the last morsel of food in a dish. Among less intimate company, people won't want to be seen finishing off a dish themselves. But if you're with close friends? Go for it.

Once the food is in your bowl, make sure you finish it. Wasting food (which is a bad look in and of itself) makes you seem ungrateful.

Oh, and be prepared to graciously field a barrage of compliments on your chopstick prowess. Whether or not they're actually impressed, your hosts might still gape at you as if you're a sorcerer.

More rules on dining etiquette are listed in Chapter 6.

GIFT-GIVING

Besides the fact that the Vietnamese are generally good-hearted and appreciative, there's the underlying belief that giving presents endows both the giver and the recipient with karmic benefits. And so gifts are given in Vietnam all the time: On birthdays, anniversaries, right before Tet (the Vietnamese New Year's Day), whenever someone comes back from a trip… or just because.

If you work or study with the locals, they'll give you gifts all the time. When someone hands you one, ask them if they prefer that you open it right then, or if you should wait for later. If it's food, they may want you to sample it. When accepting a gift, Vietnamese people will thank you over and over, but may set it aside to open later, in private.

Don't wrap gifts in black paper. This will bring up images of death and funerals. Go for red or blue instead. And if you're trying to woo someone, remember purple usually signals romantic intent.

After a trip, it's good form to bring back a small souvenir for each of your colleagues — or at least those whom you work with closely. Foreign snacks (candy or chocolates) or anything else that's not on the local store shelves are surefire winners. Tea bags, ground coffee, and even soap are good ideas. At the end of the day, what matters is the idea that you had your colleagues in mind while you were gone.

I arrived in Vietnam as an egocentric Westerner, not at all in the habit of being so consistently considerate. In my past life, when I lived in America, handing out a batch of gift cards each Christmas season was the full extent of my generosity.

There's a barista in Hanoi whom I see almost every day, and one day during small talk at the counter I mentioned that I'd just come back from visiting Danang. "So, where's my gift?" he asked, before laughing it off.

I'm pretty sure he was only half-joking.

Looking back, I should have known better; my students brought me food every time they returned from a trip. The clues were there all along, but I, the inept cultural detective, didn't pick up on them.

CHAPTER 5

SETTLING INTO THE COUNTRY

A hermit is simply someone to whom civilization has failed to adjust itself.

— Will Cuppy, journalist

GETTING IN

You'll probably need a visa to enter Vietnam, but the shifting tides of international diplomacy are changing the visa procedures all the time. Beyond that, the process of receiving one depends on some variables, such as where you're from and what you'll be doing in Vietnam.

Here's some of the most current information on getting through the border. Just remember that the rules could change tomorrow, depending on some treaty or agreement between your country and Vietnam.

Work Permit

If you're coming to Vietnam for a professional posting, then your company will probably help you through the work permit process. Work permits are valid for three years, and are good for multiple entries into the country. They can be renewed after the three years have elapsed. Documentation proving that your company needs you in-country for a long-term project might be required at that point, but just cross that bridge when you come to it.

It's possible to acquire the permit before you even get on the plane, through the Vietnamese embassy in your country. You can also apply for a work permit from within Vietnam. For that, you first enter the country on a tourist visa (more on that below) and then submit your application at the nearest office of the Department of Labour. The government says you'll receive your permit within 10 days if you application is approved, but don't hold them to that. Expats can wait for up to a month.

Note: Talk to your employer to see if you need a work permit. A recent governmental decree allows some foreigners to work in Vietnam without a work permit if they have a relevant Bachelor's Degree and a minimum of three years' experience in their respective field of work.

If you're an international hobo, as I am, then a tourist visa is your ticket in. You can apply for one at any Vietnamese

Getting a Work Permit

Expats seeking a work permit must be:
- At least 18 years of age,
- Physically fit to work,
- In possession of "skills or career expertise not available in the Vietnamese labour market",
- Able to pass a background check.

The documents you'll need will probably include the following—but don't be surprised if they ask for more:
- Notarized background check from your home country (In my case, I got it at the federal level, from the FBI),
- Health check certificate (which you get from an authorized hospital in Vietnam),
- Notarized copies of your diplomas, certifications, and certificates,
- Employer's business certification (your Vietnamese boss should know what this is),
- Employment contract,
- Passport photos (one or two, depending on where you apply),
- Copy of your passport.

If possible, bring all the notarized copies of pertinent documentation with you from your home country.

For the most current details, go to the website of the Vietnamese Ministry of Foreign Affairs: https://visa.mofa.gov.vn/ (yes, it's in Vietnamese—but don't throw your coffee mug at the wall just yet; there's an English language option on the top right of the page). You can also click over to the website of the Vietnamese embassy in your country.

Getting A Residence Card

There are two residence card options: temporary and...? Any guesses? Did you say permanent? Good job, you're correct.

You might qualify for a temporary residence card if you're a student, lawyer, business owner or board member of certain companies operating in Vietnam.

Some of the documents you'll be asked to provide are:

- Written request (known as Form N7A) for a TRC (temporary residence card),
- Declaration of information on foreigners applying for a TRC (Form N7B),
- Two passport photos,
- Copy of your passport and current visa,
- Copy of your work permit, if applicable.

And the fee will be somewhere between US$60 and US$100.

What about staying in Vietnam forever?

You can get a permanent residence card if you're the spouse (congratulations!) or immediate family member of a Vietnamese citizen living in the country. Getting one of those involves, among other things, showing the whole royal flush of birth certificates, passports and marriage licenses of all parties involved. You'll have to get the card renewed every three years.

---

embassy — but that's not even really necessary. There are dozens of visa agency websites that you can attain one through.

Doing passport-related business through a website might seem tenuous and unreliable, but it does work. Just employ a little common sense and drop by TripAdvisor or another travel site to make sure the visa site isn't a scam. I can personally vouch for these two websites:

- vietnamvisapro.net
- myvietnamvisa.com

From there, you can request a visa online, and you'll receive it upon arrival in the airport in Vietnam.

Visa-on-Arrival Process

After you fill out your application and pay the processing fee (it depends on which site you choose, but it shouldn't run you more than US$20–30), the online agency will email you an "invitation letter", which is just a travel manifest with your name (and the names of other travellers passing through the airport that day) on it.

You print the invitation letter out and fill in the visa application they should also send you. Then bring your paperwork, passport and stamping fee to the immigration counter when you arrive at the airport in Vietnam. They'll paste the tourist visa into your passport there. As for the stamping fee, it'll range from US$20–50 (it'll depend on the duration of the visa you're getting.) The visa agency will inform you exactly how much the fee will be when they email you the invitation letter.

For the most updated fee schedule, check online (www.myvietnamvisa.com/vietnam-visa-cost.html). The fee must be presented in cash, and has to be in either VND or US$. Since it's pretty hard to acquire VND outside of Vietnam, then you'll probably be paying in US dollars.

Citizens of most countries (not Americans; more on that below) currently have the choice between one- and three-month tourist visas. They can be either single-entry or multiple-entry— the latter is your best call if you're going to be hopping around Southeast Asia.

There are exceptions to this: citizens of about 20 countries (Japan, Italy, Thailand, the UK, are a few on this list) don't need to bother with that whole process I just outlined. They can get into the country and stay without a visa for around 15 days. Just do your homework, and you'll be fine.

If You Happen to Be an American...

... your only option for a tourist visa is now a one-year, multiple entry visa that costs you US$135 at the immigration counter. This arrangement is based on a recent (August 2016) deal with the Vietnamese government. What if you're just passing through Vietnam for 24 hours and want to partake in a quick bowl of *pho*? You still need a one-year visa. (This, my friends, is diplomacy in action.)

The one-year visa is a good break for long-term immigrants, because it saves you from paying the fees and submitting the paperwork necessary to re-up your tourist visa every 90 days. But every convenience has a catch: You still need to leave the country every 90 days, though (the visa's "staying duration" is listed as 90 days, despite the visa itself being good for a full year).

Why? I have tried, and failed, to find the rationale for this. Perhaps the powers-that-be keep the ground underneath our feet hot in order to remind us that we're still tourists, and that we're not here to stay. For more on this, you can check this site: www.vietnamvisa-easy.com/how-to-get-a-vietnam-visa/how-to-get-a-vietnam-visa-for-us-citizens

In-Country Visa Extension

If you're going to need a little more time on the clock, you can extend your tourist visa from within the country. A lot of travel agencies and tour companies on the streets offer the service—"Visa Extension" will be listed on the sign outside.

Make sure you have at least seven days of validity left on your visa before you file for an extension, to give the slow wheels of bureaucracy time to churn through the process. Go into the office with scans of your passport and your current visa.

This will save you from the annoying chore of having to pull a quick visa run to Bangkok or the like (which usually requires hopping on a plane there, only to get on another plane to fly right back to Vietnam). But a visa extension is not the cheapest thing; prices depend on how much more time you want to stay in Vietnam. My friend needed another 25 days in the country, and she paid US$95 for it.

(the wording is hard to follow, but the information in the tables is useful).

Reading all of this information probably gave you a headache. I (along with every other expat, I assume) was also confused when I sat down to decipher the maze keeping me from the Immigration counter.

Vietnam is currently losing ground in the tourism sector to neighbouring Cambodia, Laos and Thailand. In those countries, there are fewer thickets of red tape to be hacked through at the border. Vietnam turns off a lot of would-be adventurers by requiring them to research the visa process so thoroughly.

Life on a "Tourist" Visa

What if you feel like throwing caution to the wind and coming to Vietnam, but you have no housing or employment lined up? Get on the plane anyway. Here's the dirty secret: Even as a tourist, you can get an apartment and a job, and stay in Vietnam until the cows come home.

Tourists are not supposed to be employed here (at least, not for more than 90 days), and can technically be deported for working. But I've never heard of someone actually suffering a consequence for doing so, and neither have any of my friends.

I arrived in Hanoi as a tourist and had no plans, no job, and no place to live—but I knew I wanted to stay for a little while, so I could feel the place out. Within two days I'd signed for an apartment, and within a month I'd started working as an English tutor. And that's how most expats do it; at this particular point in history they're able to just paratroop into the city and start making a little money. How long this relative anarchy will last, however, is anyone's guess.

An American friend of mine has been managing an office in Hanoi for the past three years, and he's been using single-entry tourist visas the entire time. He'll fly over to Singapore or Bangkok for a weekend visa run, then jump back into Vietnam on a new tourist visa to reset the 90-day countdown.

An oft-travelled visa run destination is Vientiane, capital of Laos. From Hanoi, it's a 20-hour bus trip. It's a trip that can get as gritty, sleep-deprived and authentic as it's possible to get—a good fit for backpackers, but perhaps not the kind of journey you'd like to take the kids on.

But for the moment, it's currently in Vietnam's financial interest to let the tourists roll in. The service sector (hotels, transport, guided tours, etc.) is the engine pushing the economy. If the bright minds over at Immigration can figure out how to demystify the visa process and cut down on fees, they'll reap even greater rewards.

FINDING A PLACE

Other than moving from the second floor of my childhood home down to the basement, setting up digs in Vietnam was actually the smoothest move I've ever made. I landed in Hanoi on a Friday, and by Sunday I'd found a place.

Type "housing agencies in Vietnam" into Google and your computer might explode as it tries to serve you all the results. The supply is out there.

If the website is in English, you're probably on the right path. I emailed a few agencies before I arrived, and used their responses to gauge which would be a good realtor to work with. Most of them have that proactive drive that comes from the pursuit of a commission, and they'll email you when you're in town to set up a rendezvous. If you don't have your own transportation yet, they'll throw you on the back of their bike and take you on a tour of the properties.

The realtor who helped get me set up in my apartment was helpful to such a level that would seem insane back in the West. Even though she was leaving the housing agency to take another job, she texted me to let me know that she would still be available to help act as a liaison between me and the agency, in case there were any issues. Although that would be work she'd be doing off the clock, she still viewed assisting her past clients as a necessary responsibility.

Often, a property owner will designate an entire building or house for expats. These might be newer structures and have a few conveniences thrown in, like padlocked gates, elevators, and a guarded lobby, that create sort of a mini-embassy feel for those who want a little separation from the streets. Those features are comparative luxuries here, in a country with old cities comprised of old houses.

But you can rent for much, much cheaper, if you're willing to rough it and live in a walk-up in an older house. My first

Leasing as a Tourist?

As you have probably already inferred, you can sign an apartment lease even on a tourist visa. Because it's not the visa that matters—housing agencies and building managers don't seem to care much about them. What they do care about is money, and so long as you put down a deposit and let them photocopy your passport and visa then everyone will be happy.

What happens is that certain agencies pay a fee to the police in exchange for hosting foreigners. It's not hard to find a cooperative agency, because they don't have much reason to worry. They carry the risk because they know that if you run out in the middle of the night, they keep the deposit. That's fine with them; they can have the place re-rented by next Tuesday.

At contract signing, all I needed was:

- Passport,
- Visa,
- Cash for the deposit and first month's rent.

An Inconvenient Loophole

My main piece of advice to you on housing is to check your contract carefully. Nothing is a given.

During the rainy season, a wall in my apartment took on some water damage after a typhoon. The wall never dried, and was left with yellow and black stains from floor to ceiling. Pretty soon a few spots of black mold began to grow. I didn't want to get sick from breathing in mold spores, so I kept asking the housing agency to have someone come take a look at the wall.

They said they'd get on it, but never actually did. A month rolled by, and I took the contract over to the housing agency. I had already highlighted the verbiage in the contract which stated that the agency was responsible for repairing any damage to the property. Armed with this trump card, I proudly slapped the document down on the table.

The building manager nodded sympathetically and read what I'd highlighted.

"But," she eventually said, "it doesn't say when we have to fix the damage."

I checked the article on the contract again, and she was right. There was no timeline spelled out for repairs. Theoretically, they had the contractual wiggle room to wait until the last week of the lease to fix it.

place was an apartment in a modern building but when I moved out and took a room in a walk-up, I cut my rent in half.

Housekeeping

No matter where you rent, there will probably be a housekeeping service. How often your place is cleaned will depend on the arrangement you have with the landlord (the higher the rent, the more often you get your place cleaned).

In the house where I live now, a maid cleans the stairways and common areas, and takes out the trash three times a week. Depending on where you live, the housekeeping staff might also clean your bedroom. Keep your cash and valuables locked up, or at least hidden away so well that even a cop with a warrant wouldn't find them.

Almost 100% of the time, your belongings will be fine—but there are always exceptions. A friend of mind had the money for her rent payment hidden in her dresser drawers, and came home one day to find the cash gone. The maid who worked at the house denied she took the money, but she was really the only person who could have done so. The money was never recovered, the maid was reassigned to another house, and the case remains open and unsolved, as they say.

Accommodation

Most urban Vietnamese make their homes in tall buildings—well, "tall" is relative. They're not towers, but instead structures that look like houses, only stretched vertically a little bit, as if by a funhouse mirror. The emphasis is on height, since expanding horizontally would entail buying up more streetfront property and paying more in taxes. Therefore, most buildings rise five or six storeys above the street—and nearly every home is a walk-up.

With respect to spatial efficiency, entire neighbourhoods of buildings are jammed directly next to each other, and it seems that a single fire starting in one home would be enough to burn down the whole block.

Vietnamese homes are something of an optical illusion, because once you're inside, space isn't a problem. Ceilings will probably be higher and stairways wider than you expect. In other news, Vietnam is light on bathtubs and many homes have the typical Asian bathroom setup, where the shower head is placed on the wall above the toilet, and you soak the entire room along with yourself during every shower.

Another domestic feature is the Buddhist altar. Modern

apartments probably won't have them, but in older houses, it's a given. The altar might take up an entire staircase landing, or there will be a room dedicated to it. Another nearly ubiquitous fixture is the portrait of Uncle Ho. He'll be on the wall close by the altar, if not directly above it.

Gates and Guardians

Cast-iron gates protect most homes from the crime of the streets. It's a little annoying to unlock and then re-latch the gate every single time you step out, but if you don't, your home will likely be looted in short order.

Some complexes and apartment buildings have within their employ an on-site doorman/security guard. It's a selling point for a lot of properties. There was an old man who lived in the lobby of my first apartment, and was at his post 24/7. He'd seal off the building every night at midnight by rolling down a metal shutter over the garage.

We slept easy, knowing the place was secure — but building tenants weren't given keys to unlock the shutter. This meant that if I ever had a late one, my only way to get inside was to ring the bell and wake the old man up when I got back. It's true that being rousted from a deep, woozy sleep was part of his job description, but I don't think he was being paid enough to make the rude awakenings worth it.

If you end up in a place with a doorman, bring him a gift of a *banh mi* sandwich every now and then.

Blackouts

It's almost midnight and you're peacefully wandering down rabbit holes of Recommended Videos on YouTube — and then, in an instant, the lights and the AC snap off. You open the curtains and see that the whole block has gone dark.

Blackouts are probably going to hit out of left field every now and then. The power grid, only recently upgraded from a third world system, still needs a little more TLC, and maintenance is undertaken at odd hours. (And unless you've got a really hands-on landlord, don't expect a warning beforehand.)

The more lavish hotels and buildings will have probably have generators, but your home — if you're living among the people — will probably not.

I've been blacked out twice in Hanoi and once in Saigon. Every time, the power has stayed off until morning. Just keep your phone and laptop charged up, and buy a flashlight. And open a window, because you're in for a long, hot night.

Smoke and Fire

When I moved into a shared house, I didn't check it for smoke alarms — I was accustomed to accommodations that had them, so I just assumed their presence was a given.

Then, one morning this past winter, a housemate of mine fell asleep with a space heater on her bed. Being that blankets are more combustible than not, she woke up to find her bedding on fire.

Everyone fled the house in their pyjamas and joined the crowd that was forming in the alley outside. Several neighbours hustled up to our house in short order, toting buckets and fire extinguishers. We formed a line on the landing outside the burning room, crouched under the smoke and tried to contain the flames. It took us about 10 minutes, punctuated by the use of as many fire extinguishers, to kill the blaze. The damage was limited to just that one room, but the fire could have easily spread to the stairwell and burned out the rest of the house. (Take note that most houses in Vietnam do not have fire escapes.)

It'll be hard to fully relax from now on considering the fire department's response time: They didn't arrive until a full half-hour after our friendly neighbourhood gang of amateurs had done their job for them.

Your lodgings here can be cheap, but you get what you pay for. Don't be afraid to ask the landlord basic safety questions before you take the keys.

GETTING CONNECTED
Cell Phones

When my friends in America Skype me, they usually complain about money, and I usually respond by telling them to move over here. Life in the West can be expensive. In Vietnam, it's the absolute opposite; you can get cell phone service for about US$5 a month.

Getting a SIM card will be the easiest chore you'll perform upon arrival, and hopefully it'll give you the confidence you'll need to attack the more daunting tasks of immersion. What you do is walk into a small street shop with an advertisement for SIM cards posted outside (the wording in Vietnamese is *sim the*).

How you do you find one of these shops? You don't, you just trip into one. They're everywhere. Many of the little roadside vendor carts on city sidewalks will have SIM cards for sale (along with all the other necessities — water bottles, beer, umbrellas and *banh mi* sandwiches. Coming across one of these carts feels like reaching a supply stash in a video game).

The SIM card and a Vietnamese phone number should run you around 50,000 VND (US$2.50). The easiest way is to buy a month's worth of data for 100,000 VND (US$5). You load up your phone by following the instructions and typing in the code on the back of the card into your phone. It should give you a sufficient amount of data for browsing Facebook and YouTube. Different service providers provide different amount of minutes for domestic and international phone calls.

If you're a millennial like me who's afraid of phone calls, and clings to texting at all costs, then you'll be fine. You can't run out of the minutes that you don't even use. If you're the type who needs the warmth of another person's voice, then

you can drop into a corner store to recharge your minutes if you run out.

You can get the SIM card installed and recharge your credit without speaking any Vietnamese, because most shopkeepers are used to performing the connection ritual for data-starved backpackers going through withdrawals. Just remember which day it was you charged up your phone's data, so you can buy more 30 days later.

Service Providers

Vietnam has a few principal cell phone carriers: Viettel, Vinaphone and Mobiphone. Advertisements outside the shops will usually list which carrier's SIM cards they have in stock.

There's a pretty big variance between service quality—and I can make a recommendation as to which carrier you should use. Right now, I use Mobiphone, but I'm eyeing a switch to Viettel. That's the network that's owned and administered by the Vietnamese Ministry of Defence. Since the military requires high-calibre communicational capability, Viettel's service runs pretty quick. My friend has it, and while we were hiking in the jungle a few months back, he was holding a smooth, no-lag Skype call with his family back home. As for me, I couldn't even get Google Maps to refresh.

Cell Phone Etiquette

The Vietnamese have glommed to the global materialization of cell phones just as quickly as everyone else. It's a new bonding activity for the whole family to sit in Highlands Coffee and try out Snapchat filters on each other. ("Let's see the dog ears on Grandma one more time!")

Everyone else is FaceTiming on their iPads, sans headphones, so you can hear the other side of the call as well. Lucky you! And when they're sitting nearby, playing one of those games with exploding jewels, the volume is all the way up.

Bearing these vignettes in mind, it's hard to think of something you could possibly do while being engaged with a technological device that could be considered rude. The rule in the city seems to be "I'll never see you again, so why do I care what you think?"

New York would be proud.

Landlines and the Internet

In Vietnam landlines will be bundled with Internet and television. Your realtor should help you set up your connections ahead of your move-in date. Just make sure you're thorough and ask for exactly what you want. If you're going about installation by yourself, there are two major providers: Vietnam Posts and Telecommunications Group (reach their customer service line at 700), and our old friend Viettel (reachable at 19008198). They should have staff who speak English. Foreigners need their passport, visa, proof of residence and, in some cases, proof of employment on hand in order to receive service.

Your Internet service at home will be Wi-Fi by default, so let your realtor know if you want an Ethernet connection. As you probably guessed, you can get Wi-Fi in most cafés and eateries. In the cities, the newer buses let you get connected while you're on board. Surfing speed will be adequate most of the time. But the Internet is still subject to state control and will suffer from bugs in the infrastructure, so there will be days when it'll lag.

Censorship

What's all this about state control, you ask?

Vietnam has its own homegrown imitation of Big Brother. Quite afraid of the power a webpage can wield, he selectively blocks access to the subversive by using what's called the "Bamboo Firewall".

Vietnam has, only recently, reluctantly embraced the social tsunami that is Facebook. The networking hub has been unofficially blocked since about 2009 (the government never made an announcement regarding said unblocking), but citizens were getting their dopamine fix with VPNs anyway.

In case you're new to this Bond-ian existence of circumventing government oppression with a laptop, a VPN (Virtual Private Network) masks your IP address so that you appear to be accessing the web from a different country. Downloading a VPN will open up the Internet for you upon the occasion of the next crackdown.

There are about a million free VPNs online available for download, but Google Chrome's Hola extension is an option, should you need it. And you might yet; in May 2016, Facebook was inaccessible for a weekend. The reason? That was the weekend when Vietnamese citizens were using the platform to organize protests against the government's (perceived lack of) response to a corporation's chemical spill that killed off millions of fish.

Of course, there are other websites on the Internet. I've found bbc.co.uk blocked a few times as well.

I haven't heard of a foreigner landing himself in hot water (read: jail) due to online activity (as you can in Thailand, for tweeting anything unsavoury about the King). But as recently as fall 2016, some local bloggers were still being arrested and having their sites blacked out for posting content critical of the state.

The rule here seems to be the same as it is in, well, every nation that's not branded as a democracy: You'll be all right, as long as you don't cause too much of a ruckus.

SHOPPING

Let's double back to the motif of cheap living for a second: Every time my motorbike tank runs dry, I fill it up for just 60,000 VND (US$2.50), and when I grab a street beer after work, I pay 5,000 VND (US$0.25) per can. This is the cost of living in Vietnam—much lower than what I was used to back home.

But it's not all good news—where you spend your money determines its value. If you end up living in a foreigner's enclave, like Hanoi's Tay Ho or Saigon's Districts 2 and 7, then you'll be able to alleviate any homesickness by paying those familiar high Western prices for your meals and groceries. I made the mistake of doing my move-in shopping at a more "upscale" market called FiviMart in Hanoi, where all the bankers and foreign officials shop. Furnishing a small apartment with kitchen and bathroom essentials set me back over US$400, around double what my research had let me to expect.

Don't worry—there are other options, just in case you're

What to Bring from Home

Even though Vietnam is modernizing, it'll still always be a reality that's slightly askew from the one you came from. There are going to be certain imported products that will be quadruple the price you'd expect them to be. That's if you can find them at all—some things are so hard to find here that you could hold a devious scavenger hunt based around the collection of them.

Note that you'll have more luck shopping for your specific Western comforts in Saigon than Hanoi.

- **Soap, Moisturizer and Sunscreen:** Vietnamese like their skin as Casper-white as possible, so their skincare products have enough whitening agents in them to get you looking like Michael Jackson by the end of your first month. On my visa runs, I buy refills of the basics and carry them back into 'Nam.

- **Electronics**: Cameras, computers and peripherals will come at a higher cost if they've been imported. You may need to chase down a two-pronged 220V voltage adapter. Whether you buy it here or at home, it won't cost you much.

- **Kitchen Goods**: Vietnamese cuisine doesn't require as many tools and utensils to prep as the multi-coursed fare us complicated foreigners eat. So if you want a pizza peel, French press, rolling pin or juicer—you should bring them from home, unless you are willing to pay a king's ransom for them here (those are pricey here). Ask yourself if the item in question is used in Vietnam to cook a local meal, and if the answer is no, then it might be worth to pack and ship it, if you have the extra cargo space.

- **Footwear and Clothing**: Bring what you need and like to wear, especially if you're uniquely proportioned in any way. I'm 200cm tall, and the only garments I've been able to purchase in Vietnam have been socks and T-shirts (oh, and those stretchy elephant pants). Anything that's larger than life won't be on sale here.

- **Camping Gear**: This is not cheap here. If you're outdoorsy at all, you'll be glad you came prepared.

- **Medication**: The more you can get over here, the better—in case there's any snafus with filling your prescription in a Vietnamese pharmacy.

the kind of person who doesn't enjoy throwing money around like you're starring in a rap video.

Where Should I Shop?

For groceries and everything else you need for the home, look up Big C. It's pretty much a Vietnamese Costco or Wal-mart and there are stores throughout the country. What I do is take my hiking backpack over there and fill it up with groceries for the week. The store is noisy, it can be hard to locate a staff member to direct you to the right aisle, and its crowds bring to mind images of a post-apocalyptic evacuation, but it's got all the basics. Not all of the signage will be in English though, so prepare to do some exploring.

Lotte Mart is an establishment similar to Big C, and has superstores in both Hanoi and Saigon. At both Big C and Lotte supermarkets, you'll pay about half of what you would at the shiny import stores.

Some of your eyebrows may have risen at the use of the word "import"—maybe you're in the market for some elusive items such as gourmet cheeses, aged wines, maple syrup, seasonings, etc. But if you want to go cheaper, local grocery stores are easy to find. And most city blocks host small mom-and-pop operations (the same stores you can pick up SIM cards at) with the basics: rice, cereal, milk, crackers and household items.

If you're in Hanoi you can look up:
- L's Place (there are shops in both Hoan Kiem and Tay Ho District),
- Hanoi Gourmet (Hoan Kiem District),
- The Oasis Grocery Store & Gourmet Shop (Tay Ho District).

And here's a list for Saigon. It's longer, because Saigon has more of everything:

- Annam Gourmet Market (District 1),
- Diamond Plaza Select Mart (District 1),
- Thai Hoa (District 1),
- Veggy's (District 1),
- Vincom Centre Select Mart (District 1),
- The Organik Shop (District 2),
- River Garden Select Market (District 2).

All-Night Shopping

There are few chains of 24-hour convenience stores in Vietnam: Circle K, Shop & Go and Family Mart.

Learn where the closest one is to you, because there will be times you'll need something after midnight and nothing else will be open. Hanoi, unsurprisingly, only has a handful of these stores, while Saigon has scores of them.

Produce

The local markets in the city are the cheapest way to obtain on fruits and vegetables. The vendors will be amused to see you in a spot off the beaten track, and it'll be a good chance to practice a few phrases of Vietnamese.

In Hanoi, I recommend the huge night market that's set up under Long Bien Bridge. In Saigon, where there are far more grocery stores scattered about, you can head over to Ba Chieu Market, in Binh Thanh District.

Markets and Haggling

Some guests I've hosted here had seen scenes of hardball negotiation in the movies and were itching to live out their own version of it. When you're ready for the open market experience, plot a course for Saigon's Ben Thanh Market for shopping and street food (look for crab noodle soup, called *banh canh cua*).

Ben Thanh is in District 1, and it's the site of what I call the Haggling Olympics. Practice your polite "no thanks" smile because you'll need it. And in case you've never done this before, go into each negotiation with a very low price, because they'll be coming in with an astronomically high one.

Besides about 100 million other street shops, Saigon also has Dan Sinh. That's the war surplus market, for those of you whose fashion sense trends toward "combat chic".

If you want to haggle for street merch in Hanoi, go to Hoan Kiem Lake in the Old Quarter. On the north end, near the traffic circle, there are dozens of little shops and stalls. They've got T-shirts branded with slogans from the revolution, rice hats, green hats with the Communist star on them, fans with calligraphy, silk pyjama pants and everything else you've seen in Facebook travel albums.

Find what you want and name your price. When they balk, just keep playing the game by walking away. The stall next door will be selling the same exact goods, so you can play them off each other and keep driving the price down.

Streetside Economy

The economy is such that street hustlers are everywhere, and they will be bold. They'll port around their wares (scarves, gum, tissues, donuts — literally anything) in a basket, or by strapping a sandwich board-type contraption to their torsos.

Other street sellers carry fruit or bread in baskets balanced on either end of bamboo shoulder poles. If you don't want what they're selling, they'll offer you something else — the

A Vietnamese woman hikes the road under the weight of a shoulder pole laden with goods.

chance to pose with their (really, really heavy) pole on your shoulder while you wear their rice hat. People who fall for this, no doubt because they've already mentally tabulated the Facebook likes the photo will reap, will then be asked by the seller for money.

To me, it's amazing to consider the dozen of generations of thin, hardworking, tough-spirited Vietnamese women have carried these shoulder poles, sometimes weighted with upwards of 30kg of goods, day in and day out for the majority of their lives.

Around the Old Quarter in Hanoi, a lot of goods are grouped by street, where almost every business on the stretch of road is a carbon copy of its neighbour and sells the same goods. For example, I bought a camera on "Camera

Street" and a guitar on "Guitar Street." You get the idea. I can't imagine how all the shops stay financially afloat in this unique iteration of capitalism, but luckily for you, the competition puts downward pressure on prices.

Now, names like "Fabric Street" or "Jewellery Street" aren't official street names (surprise) but with some quick Google recon, you can figure out the Viet name of the street you're looking for.

The Creative Hustlers

You'll meet a few beggars with boldly creative stories. A handicapped woman ventured up to my friend and me once, and said she'd lost a leg in the American War. I asked how old she was, and she told me she was 35.

I almost expressed my astonishment at the fact she'd somehow suffered an injury no sooner than a decade after the Americans shipped out, but the angel on my shoulder won out and I gave her 5,000 VND instead.

Vendors will come up to your table in the restaurant, or shadow you through the city for a block or two even after you've waved them off. I guess they do this just in case you change your mind and decide you do actually want some beads and bangles. Families who can't afford to send their children to school will conscript them into the family business, and send them around the streets selling chewing gum.

A lot of vendors are undeterred by both the word and the general concept of "no" and will present you with a supply even when there's no demand. I've formed this hypothesis because every time I walk around downtown wearing sunglasses, I'm offered a pair of sunglasses. And shoe-shiners, carrying their tell-tale blue plastic baskets, will approach and motion to your feet to ask if you want a polish.

Once, when a friend and I were wandering around near the mountain town of Sapa, a local woman approached and offered us some jewelry. We declined, and then hiked through a village and around the rice paddies for an hour.

She stayed with us the whole time.

"But sir, are you sure you don't want a bracelet for your wife? Sister? Mother?"

And so on. (Points must be awarded for persistence.)

Hanoi at 5pm: All revved up with nowhere to go.

PUBLIC TRANSPORT
Traffic

Before we zoom in on any specific modes of transport, I'd be remiss in my duties as your advance man here in Vietnam if I didn't give you the thorough rundown on traffic.

In the countryside and smaller cities, the roads are quieter—but that doesn't mean they're better. They have enough potholes to rival the surface of the moon.

But those obstacles can be handled. What you'll end up having issues with is the lack of traffic enforcement in urban Vietnam, and the recklessness that blooms in this vacuum. Most motorbikers, unfortunately emboldened, shoot out of blind drives without slowing. When they're not doing that, they stage kamikaze attacks on you by driving the wrong way up a one-way road.

Many intersections in Hanoi's Old Quarter don't have stop lights, leading to a free-for-all demolition derby every time you move another block up the grid. There's only one rule: The biggest vehicle wins.

All of that deals with moving traffic. But traffic stops, too.

Easily and often. The country's population has outgrown its network of thin, crumbling roads, and it doesn't take too many motorbikes to cork up the streets.

After experiencing the rush-hour gridlock in both Los Angeles and pre-Big Dig Boston, I can attest that they have nothing on Vietnam. Traffic jams here are purgatorial experiences, and the only remedy for them is creative scheduling. Example: If I have a meeting at 6pm, I'll leave the house obscenely early, arrive two hours before I actually need to and do some work in a nearby café until showtime.

Now, the traffic isn't always a curse. As the police seem to care little for enforcing traffic rules, there's a lot you can get away with if you're late and your patience is running thin. Consider the sidewalk. It pulls double duty as an extra traffic lane, and using it to cut around a knot of congestion is a common traffic hack. Have I done this? Well, I don't want my editor to balk at being associated with any perilous advice, so I'll just plead the fifth on this one.

If you're going to be commuting in Hanoi or Saigon, take heart — the cavalry is on the horizon. One reason the traffic is so bad in those cities is that they've torn up a few major roads to construct their inaugural metro lines. Hanoi should open two lines in 2018, and Saigon plans to follow suit by 2020.

City Buses

Too petrified to get on a bike? I give you the city bus, your one and only public transport option in urban Vietnam. The largest cities (those include Hanoi, Saigon, Can Tho, Haiphong, and Danang) all have bus lines. Riding one from A to B may well turn into a long, ponderous journey, but the biggest positive is that you're shielded from the potential impact of any road wrecks.

The buses themselves are clearly numbered, and a few of their major stops should be listed on a sign on the vehicles' front or rear. The fares will be printed on the side of the bus (on one of the windows, up near the front doorway.) Fares usually go from 5,000 to 10,000 VND, depending on how far you're going. The airport bus will probably be 30,000 VND.

Out in the sticks, bus stops can be pretty barebones installations—sometimes it'll just be a sign on a pole, jammed into the pavement, so you can't always count on a big city map with the bus routes marked. Within the city proper, the bus stops have been given a little more TLC.

I get a little confused looking up bus routes online, as it's hard to find up-to-date timetables. But you can always type your route into Google Maps, which should give you current intel on where the best stops are, how long the trip will take, and what the aggregate fare should be. Note that the bus schedules and routes tend to be adjusted around the New Year, so it's worth checking your route again after 1 January.

One more thing—Buses occasionally double as training grounds for pickpockets, so watch yourself and your things when you're on board.

City Taxis

The only times I'll take a taxi in Vietnam are when 1) I'm trying to move cargo that's simply impossible to haul by motorcycle and… that's it. There is no 2).

If you can get on a scooter or motorbike and take control of your own destiny, that's usually the better option. Because while you're cosily shielded from the smog and tropical sun when you're sitting inside a car, the drawback is that you're at the mercy of the bikes, flowing around you like a river current. They're manoeuvrable, and you're not—the city roads weren't designed for Ford Rangers.

Taxis are a better bet by night, when traffic thins. There are a few major companies running cabs in the cities, and there's not much variance between the fares.

But there are some points you should be aware of. Cabbies commonly futz with their meters so they spin faster than normal. You won't be able to figure this out on your first few rides, before you develop an instinct for what the distance-to-fare ratio should be. But once you've gotten the lay of the land, just have the driver stop the cab if you see the meter's running on fast-forward.

It's annoying, but remember to keep a lid on it. Just pay the damage, bail, and hail a new ride. Getting angry won't solve the problem. With a number of taxi drivers being dissatisfied with their careers and having their patience ground down to the nub (battling traffic from dusk till dawn will do that to you), don't be surprised if their patience rests on a hair trigger. A few friends of mine have gotten into shoving matches.

Also, beware of getting the run-around. The cabbies assume you don't know the city, and more than a few of them will try to mine a higher fare out of you if they think they can swing it.

I went on a run on my first night in the city, to try to build a mental map of the Old Quarter, where I was staying. This actually paid off the next day — I was in a cab heading north, but when our taxi driver picked us up he immediately pointed the cab south. I pulled out a screenshot of the city from Google Maps, affected deep confusion, and politely asked him to turn around. His expression was a mix of "Damn,

If you are put off by the concept of taking a city cab, don't worry. You've got fallbacks. Uber, Lyft, and Grab all work here, and they have bike options as well.

foiled again," and "No worries, I'll run the same play on the next passengers."

Now, there are silver linings. You can work their unscrupulous mindsets to your advantage by negotiating an off-meter fare before you get in. When I'm rolling to the airport, I hail a cab and offer 200,000 VND. I'm happy because that's cheaper than the meter would be, and the cabbie's happy because he keeps the fare for himself.

Motorbike Taxis
No bike? No smartphone either?

There's always another way. A freelancing subset of the workforce has carved out a living offering motorbike taxi rides.

You'll see the drivers in groups, cooling their heels on busy corners, some chatting and drinking *tra da* (tea), others stretched out napping on their bike seats as if on hammocks. When they see you walking by, they'll flap a hand and call out "Moto? Moto?" These are called *xe om* (pronounced say ohm). They might have those words scrawled on a piece of cardboard in Sharpie, advertising their services.

In Saigon, where the sidewalks are broader, they'll ride up next to you, match your speed and give you their pitch over and over until you'll be tempted to jam a tree branch through their spokes.

Make sure they have a helmet for you, because they drive like bats out of hell. I'm always needled with the worry that we'll crash and that I'll end up as bean paste on the median, but the upshot of the risk is that a bike is mobile and can slice through traffic more easily than a blocky taxi can.

Negotiate with the driver and get a rate locked in beforehand. Like I said, you'll develop an instinct for what's fair. I wouldn't pay more than 10,000–15,000 VND per

A *xe om* driver takes a nap on the roadside.

kilometre. If they try to change the price at the drop-off, don't get into a discussion with them—best to just politely hand over the previously-agreed sum, and walk away.

Some hotels can hook you up with a *xe om* day tour of the city. That might be a good play for you if you want to cover a lot of ground with a native guide.

Lastly, keep your wits about you. This is a country where anything can happen. I wouldn't take a *xe om* after dark.

LEAVING THE CITY
Trains
Railways string Vietnam's big cities together. The tracks are laid atop cliffs, through the jungles and the paddies, and on the coastline around the bays. If you've got the time, this is how you should get around. The train is the clear winner when stacked against the harried procedure of being cattle-herded through 'Nam's airports.

The majority of the train cars are large, boxy constructs that bring to mind old Soviet newsreel footage. While they look fairly rickety, like they've been excavated from a junkyard and given a quick spray-paint job, they're safe and they'll get you to Danang or wherever in one piece. But are they punctual? Not especially. I always mentally tack on an hour or two when I'm on the Orient Express. Like I said, take the train if you've got the time.

Newer trains give you the option of riding in a car with AC. For your sanity, that's what you should do. Spending your trip in what'll come to feel like a rolling shipping container can turn a 12-hour journey into a small eternity.

The trains also have cramped bathrooms, and meals for sale. I'd bring my own snacks, though. And a book too, for after you've read and watched everything on the Internet.

You have a few ticket options.

- **Hard seater:** This is the cheapest way to ride, and you'll see why—these cars are filled with rigid benches jammed too close together. Don't count on much leg room. Hard seater is fine if you're just making a quick puddle jump over to the next city. But considering the general crush of humanity that's present in these cars—and all the jabbering and chain-smoking that comes with it—I really don't recommend hard seater for a long trip unless you have no other option.
- **Soft seater:** Moving right along up the pay scale: Soft seater cars are configured like their evil twin, the hard seater. But instead of a bench, you're bestowed with a reclining, vinyl-covered chair.
- **Hard sleeper:** Sleeper cars are probably the closest to the Hogwarts Express you'll ever get. If it's a long haul out to your destination, you can sleep on board in one of the cars, and wake up as the train lumbers

into the station. There will be six beds per car (three stacked on each wall). I've done this twice—and I'll do it again.

More basic info is presented in English on vietnam-railways. com

- **Soft sleeper:** Same deal as the hard sleeper, but with thicker mattresses and far more space in the train car—only four berths in every car, as opposed to six. Private trains (Livitrans, King Express and Sapaly, to name a few) bring luxury up to a level you only really see on private jets, with soft-hued wood panels walls, candles, bouquets of flowers and all sorts of other nonsense that puts you in a warm little sanctuary if travelling in Asia has gotten too real for you.

If you're going with a sleeper, there should be electric outlets in every car. Sometimes they'll be near every bed.

You can usually book your tickets online, if you have a Vietnamese bank account or an international credit card. Or you can have a travel agent help you. After your purchase is complete, you print out a voucher and then exchange it at the rail station for your actual ticket.

Sleeper berths on the popular routes sell out faster than tickets to a Taylor Swift concert, so book as far in advance as possible. Two weeks should do it, but on some lines you can purchase up to 90 days in advance.

As long as you're not bringing your entire life with you, you can bring your luggage on board and keep it under your own personal protection.

And, this being motorbike nation, you can bring your bike (or bicycle) with you and pick it up at point B. You can check it aboard the train by presenting it at the ticket office.

They'll show you where to wheel it and give you a receipt. It should cost between 350,000 and 400,000 VND. Usually you have to show up at least a few hours earlier than your departure time in order to get your bike stowed, so plan that into your schedule.

Intercity Buses

Your other option to strike out to the next city (or to Laos and Cambodia) is by bus. The best bet is to look up your exact route, and buy tickets in person at the relevant bus station or tour company office.

Private companies might operate coach buses. But those are rarer. If you're new to Asia, prepare to meet the sleeper bus. Longer journeys are almost exclusively completed using them. The inside of the bus is literally filled with beds, three rows of them, stacked two high. The back half of each mattress (where your torso rests) is angled slightly upward, and there may or may not be TV monitors on the ceiling, showing movies no one ever asked to see. A thin blanket and pillow are thrown in.

For most people, they're comfortable. My only advice is this: bring an eyeshade and noise-cancelling headphones. Oh, and don't be very tall. I'm 6 ft 7 (200cm) — maybe just ever-so-slightly larger than the passengers the designers had in mind. I don't like travelling on buses, because of my height. Even people shorter than I am lament the cramped conditions.

But, being buses, they can get you to all the tourist draws where the train tracks don't go — Ha Long Bay is one example that comes to mind.

Hotels and hostels can help book the trip for you. Their concierge (I'm not sure if hostels have someone with such a fancy job title, but you get the idea) will arrange to have a van pick you up and bring you to the bus itself. This will probably be in the morning, since most day trips require hitting the road by dawn. All you have to do is wake up and get down to the lobby in time.

Maximizing Space

When a friend and I went from Hanoi up to the mountain town of Sapa for a day hike, we took a sleeper bus. It wasn't bad — it had Wi-Fi and a bathroom (not at all buses do). The only issue was the shrieks and squeals from the contestants of Vietnamese game show the driver had playing on the TV up front. He had the audio piped through the whole bus's speaker system. We asked him if he could turn it down, and he just shook his head. All right, then. Sleeper bus in name only.

Our trip back was subpar in its own way.

In Sapa, we had a miscommunication with the guy at the ticket office, and our bus tickets ended up being for 8am the following morning, instead of 8pm that night, which was what we'd wanted. We needed to get back to Hanoi, so we tried to switch our departure time.

"Tonight, everything's booked," we were told.

So we went to the bus depot and stood in the boarding area, waiting to buy any vacant seats in case there were any no-shows.

"No seats," a driver told us. "But maybe you can buy a spot on the floor, it's cheaper."

Buses in Vietnam sell floor space in the aisles, too. If you're willing to sit on the carpet for the duration of the trip, they'll gladly take your money and let you do so.

"Maybe? Why 'maybe'?" I asked. I assumed the floor would be wide open.

"Because the floor is sold out, too," the driver said.

For a mild discount off a seat price, we did end up securing two patches of floor, and proceeded to sit Indian-style for the next six hours. This was a position in which neither of us had ever sat in for more than six minutes before.

Somewhere in the future, there's a chiropractor who's putting his kids through college thanks solely to the frequency of my appointments with him.

In my experience, even if you're not a guest, you can still call a hotel near you, ask for a seat on the bus, and then just show up at the hotel when it's time to go.

Payment varies; some places ask for it in advance, and they'll take care of the ticket purchase for you. Others say it's all right to pay at departure.

But if you're like me, and nothing less than a gunshot can convince you to get of bed before 6am, I recommend buying the ticket in advance in order to lock yourself into the trip.

PRIVATE VEHICLES

Cars

Private cars are rare, as the government hits auto buyers with prohibitive taxes and fees—although said taxes and fees are slowly being lowered (which is ominous news for Vietnam's already-overburdened roadway infrastructure). But for now, ownership of even an outdated, low-end auto speaks of financial success and disposable income.

Car ownerships creeps up each year. I'm all for having a vehicle if you have the means. (But we the people beg you to please not drive it in Hanoi—the roads are too narrow, and a wideset car plugs up the alleys and streets like a cork).

Buying a Car

As it stands now, you can purchase your own vehicle if you're here on a visa that lasts longer than three months (emphasis on "longer"), have a Vietnamese driver's licence (or an IDP converted from your domestic licence) and a valid passport—all the obvious things. Whether you buy from a dealership or go private, you have 10 days after purchase to register your car (the dealership will make sure you're aware of this).

Before registration you need to get the purchase
agreement and all the other paperwork relating to the car
purchase notarized. That paperwork will also include your
Certificate of Vehicle Inspection and proof of auto insurance.
Foreigners are expected to use the notarization services at
their respective embassies.

Then you saddle up in your new car and drive yourself
(ideally with a Vietnamese interpreter) to the nearest Traffic
Team Office and present your documents. Expat Woman
(www.expatwoman.com/vietnam/monthly_vietnam_driving.
aspx) has the addresses of the closest offices, along with a
plethora of other information related to driving in Vietnam.

And after everything's squared away, you'll have the
privilege of paying the registration and the licence plate fees.
Remember I used the word "prohibitive" when describing
auto fees earlier? That's because just these two fees alone
can add up to as much as 10% of the car's purchase price.

If you're buying a used car, you'll jump through all the same hoops. But if you're purchasing it in another province, you'll have to visit the police in your new province to re-register it there. The vehicle will also have to be inspected in your province before you can take your first legal joyride.

Renting a Car

Most rental agencies—perhaps doubling as job-placement agencies for local drivers—will only give you the option of hiring a chauffeured car. If you recoil at traversing the city under the beating sun, on a rickety scooter, during what seems to be an eternal rush hour, then this isn't that bad of a deal. Better to let someone else do the driving, so you're free to look around and take your pictures. Rates can range from US $40–100 per day, depending on the area, the make of the car, distance travelled and other variables.

You have a lot of hoops to jump through before you can rent a car without a driver. Many agencies explicitly state that

Car Inspections

The Ministry of Transport doesn't require regular inspection of motorbikes or scooters. Cars are, of course, another story. If your car is under 15 years old, it has to be inspected every 11 months. More information is located at www.angloinfo.com/how-to/vietnam/transport/vehicle-ownership/vehicle-roadworthinesss.

Parking

If you're going to a mall or apartment complex, this is pretty easy to figure out. Most parking garages are subterranean, and to access them you drive down a ramp until you encounter a little checkpoint. You'll get a paper ticket (though electronic cards have made a debut in the more upscale centres).

When you make your exit at the opposite end of the garage, you hand your ticket (or plastic card) and a few thousand dong to the guards at the checkpoint there. Rates vary, but I've never paid more than 10,000 VND.

they don't provide a "self-driving" service. They know how dangerous the roads here are, and they're cutting down on liabilities by keeping you out of the driver's seat.

If you somehow find an agency that lets you rent, they'll want to see a Vietnamese driver's licence, as well as insurance, before they give you the keys. Rental companies with international branches (think Avis or Budget) can help you lease a car as well.

Motorbike Nation

With cars unaffordable and bicycles impractical, the Vietnamese have turned to motorbikes — so, so many motorbikes. Over 40 million of them rumble up the country's roads every day. The motorbike (this book's catch-all term for automatic scooters, semi-automatic motorbikes and full-on manual motorcycles) is the two-wheeled beast of burden that carries an entire population and economy on its back.

And that's probably how you'll get around. Scooter culture has made converts of most expats. Backpackers, and ESL teachers and businessmen putter through the cities on them. The convenience of a scooter cuts across class and status, you'll see consummate professionals depart a restaurant and add the finishing touch to their three-piece suit by clipping on a scooter helmet.

The locals worship their motorbikes and all the mobility and independence they represent. They'll fire up the engine even if they're only rolling to the end of the alley. I'd insert a judgmental screed about green living here, but I find myself doing the same sometimes.

Acquiring a Motorbike

Motorbike rental shops are legion in the cities, and usually you

A typical motorbike rental shop in Hanoi.

The Scooter Savior

I rented a scooter during my first week in Vietnam, and my inaugural hour of joyriding left my nerves feeling like they'd been run through a cheese grater. I took a break and parked outside a downtown restaurant for dinner. And when I came back out, the scooter wouldn't start.

I called the bike shop, but they were closed up for the night. Up the block, I saw a truck of police crawl by. It was getting late, and it wouldn't be long before they started lifting delinquent bikes off the sidewalk and taking them off to the impound.

At the other end of the street, an old man was lounging on his bike under a streetlight. He waved at me and pointed at my scooter seat. He wanted me to get on.

"No, you don't understand," I said, frustrated I couldn't explain myself to him. "The bike is dead."

We repeated this circular exchange a few times, and he kept laughing at me and signaling, as if to say trust me, just get on the bike.

I threw up my hands and got on, making a futile show of turning the key. The old man fired up his bike and rode over. He stuck out a foot and kicked the passenger footrest of my scooter. I started rolling — and that's when I got it.

He did the work; all I had to do was steer. Whenever I decelerated, he'd give me another kick to get me back up to speed. He propelled me all the way back to my hotel, about five kilometers away. I think he'd have done it for free, but I handed him 100,000 VND at the end of the ride. He gave me a little salute and then rode away up the road, perhaps off to rescue the next godforsaken expat.

can pick up a bike for an average of a dollar a day (800,000 VND/month is standard.)

Some enterprises will even deliver the bike to your house after you call them and order one. Another upside to renting is that most shops perform free basic maintenance on your bike once a month.

Riding a (Very) Used Bike

Compounding the risk involved with frantic Vietnamese traffic is that the motorbike you rent will probably be an older, delicate contraption that's absorbed untold amounts of punishment. You'll have no idea how many expats your bike has carried before you, and monthly maintenance may not fix the deeper problems that will manifest over time.

Riding will involve some guesswork on your part, too — the speedometers and odometers on most bikes I've rented have been busted. They break easily, and the shops don't bother to fix them. I've asked shop owners for a bike with working gauges, and am always told that none are in stock.

Beyond that, there are rumours that broken motorbike parts are often quietly replaced with cheap Chinese components, which soon break again, trapping you in a vortex of wasted time as you return to the shop for repairs again and again. So take your time and browse for a new one, if you can. My suggestion is to look around for newer, trimmer models, and then test-drive a few of them to see which one rides and brakes the best.

And if you've never ridden a semi-auto or a manual motorcycle before, ask the shop owner or staff to teach you how to ride before you skid off into traffic.

If you have an older bike, don't trust the gas gauge since it'll probably be inaccurate. I'd head to a gas station

Helmets

Use of a helmet has been the law of the land for a few years now. But what exactly is a helmet?

Vendors squat on road shoulders with thin plastic brain buckets spread out on a blanket. They look exactly like baseball caps—and except for their bright sheen, they're indistinguishable from one—but they still count as a "helmet." (The Hello Kitty design is in vogue right now, and it's a hoot to see hot-rodders in leather jackets wearing one.)

These "helmets" will get you past a police checkpoint, but that's where the benefits end. They're so flimsy it's like they've been 3-D printed. If you go down and your head hits the pavement, you're only going to one of two places—the coma ward or a body bag. The plastic is simply too thin; it will crack like an eggshell.

You're going to want a real, heavy, substantial helmet. (Look for a full-face model, so you don't smash your jaw into powder). They're double the price of the thin ones, but you still probably won't pay more than US$20 for one. I'm pretty sure that's cheaper than an ICU stay.

immediately after procuring the bike keys. Most shops don't keep the bikes gassed up — that's your job.

I've run out of gas before, only to be saved by a Good Samaritan who siphoned a rubber tube full of black gold out of his own tank and funnelled it into mine.

You'll see soda bottles filled with petrol sitting out on the roadside. That's emergency fuel that the locals will sell you so you can make it to the next gas station, in case you've run out. It's tempting, but it's better to just push your bike; they water down the gas, creating a diluted solution that will wreck the engine.

Buying a Bike

Buying a bike is more cost-effective, if you know that you're going to be here for a while. Almost all bike sales are private, off-the-books, cash transactions — but you should receive a blue registration card along with the bike. If you're stopped by the cops and you don't have that card on your person, the bike could be confiscated.

There are a few ways to find a bike. Expats are constantly cycling out of the country and selling their wheels, so you might hear of a deal through word of mouth. Besides that, check the flyers on the walls outside hostels and on grocery store bulletin boards. Online, Travelswop.com should be one of your first stops. Also try joining Facebook expat groups, since not a day goes by without a scooter ad being posted. Keep an eye on Craiglist Vietnam as well.

Motorbike shops in Hanoi that sell to expats include, but are by no means limited to, the following:
- Quang Minh Motorbike,
- Hanoi Motorbike,
- Viet Motorbikes.

And in Saigon, look these up:

- Tigit Motorbikes,
- The Bike Shop,
- Saigon Scooter Centre,
- HCMC Motorbikes.

The majority of bikes in the market these days are Hondas and Yamahas. Prices for a used one aren't bad: you'll probably hand over around US$200–350. After a few months of ownership, the bike's paid for itself. Obviously, if you want something faster or flashier, or something with fewer kilometres on it, you'll pay more.

You can find an even better price if you have both the time and confidence in your Vietnamese skills. Do some recon on the local bike shops; a sign out front with the words "Xe Ban" means they're selling bikes. Get ready to haggle a little bit.

Footwear

One more thing—wear shoes when you're on your bike.

I was once waiting at a red light on my motorbike, and became aware of an incredible pressure on my right foot, growing exponentially heavier by the second. A black Mercedes had rolled up next to me and its tire was pinning my shoe to the ground. The driver had tried to squeeze between my bike and the traffic light, and ended up perching a few thousand pounds of automobile atop the thin bones of my foot.

I panicked and starting bashing the window with my fist while I screamed at him to move. The driver looked my way, took a few endless seconds to figure out what was happening, then shrugged as if to say oops, I did it again, and pulled away disappearing across the intersection.

Somehow, I was all right—but if I'd been wearing flip-flops, I'm pretty sure this story would have ended differently, with flayed skin, at the very least.

A buddy of mine had it worse; a city bus ran over his foot at a red light, leaving him with a whole mess of hairline fractures and a limp that persisted for a few weeks.

Perhaps the lightest traffic you're likely to see in urban Vietnam.

Riding in the City

Be careful. Because not only is the gridlock deeply annoying — it's lethal, too. Official government reports estimate that 15,000 Vietnamese are killed in motor accidents every year, which divides out to about 40 fatalities a day. Although it's illegal to ride without a helmet, a high number of adrenaline junkies still do without them — and they ride quickly. A subset of motorists seem to have taken their cues from action movies, only they don't have a script to ensure their survival. And such luck can dry up pretty quickly — I've twice been late to work because city workers had stopped traffic to remove a dead biker from the road.

Bikers who die because they're not wearing a helmet will sometimes be "shamed" after death by having their names printed on a city billboard.

A Nation of Stunt Riders

With ownership of an SUV or minivan a nigh-impossible dream, a family of five (seriously) will pack onto a single motorbike and gun through traffic. Aren't they scared? Not at all. They're scrolling through their Facebook feed or snacking, just as unaware of the inherent risk as fish is of water.

It's hard to be fully at ease within the madness on the streets, because even if you maintain a reasonable speed and check your surroundings, you still might get hit. Because it's not just the velocity of the other bikes that's a factor — it's what's on the bikes.

As borrowing a friend's pickup truck is a rare luxury for the locals, they just lash any and everything to their bike frames. I've seen couches, flatscreen TVs, 15-foot-long steel bars, panes of glass and crates of chickens being hauled through the streets at a considerable speed.

Just when you think you've seen the most ridiculous, reckless, dangerous traffic situation in your entire life, Vietnam pulls another rabbit out of the hat. You'll see locals driving, with their pet dogs sprinting next to them, their leashes tethered to the motorbike handlebars. What if the dog gets winded and slows down, or sees a squirrel and bolts to the side? The only possible outcome would be a nasty, multi-bike pileup. It's mildly amazing that anyone in Vietnam has survived enough a year on the streets.

One general rule of the road is that the left-hand lane is for cars, and the right is reserved for motorbikes. Break this rule if you want (everyone does) but just know that cars are completely unafraid of giving you a little bump if you're in their way.

If you're thinking that all that extra heft must make it harder for drivers to brake and turn, you'd be right. Not long ago, a young boy

A pillion bike rider carrying a large picture frame through the streets.

In Hanoi was killed when his throat was cut by a sheet of corrugated metal being carried on a bike that crashed into his.

Again: The bottom line is, be careful.

Getting a Driver's Licence

There's a few different roads to licensure. If you don't have a licence in your home country, nothing's stopping you from applying for a Vietnamese driver's licence. The wrinkle is that you'll have to do it as the Vietnamese do, with road tests and everything—and there's no English version of the test.

Hope your Vietnamese is good enough!

If you hold a licence or an International Driving Permit (IDP), you can get it converted into a Vietnamese licence.

At the minimum, you'll need a three-month tourist visa or a residence permit. Then you'll also need your passport, a notarized copy of your current driver's licence

Sidewalks

Vietnam's urban sidewalks have exploded the definition of the term mixed-use. Clothing racks, fire hydrants, café tables, keymakers and vendors have all colonized their own few precious rows of bricks. There's room for almost everything, except for pedestrians.

Somewhere in the middle of it all, there's also some motorbike parking. To keep feathers unruffled, drive up over the curb and park directly in front of the shop you're going to enter. Shopkeepers mount an aggressive defense of the real estate in front of their stoops. If they think you're going to block their cash flow by plugging up a parking spot, they'll let you know immediately via a shout and maybe a light shove.

Larger establishments will have someone watching the parking area. They might give you a numbered ticket so you can check your bike in with them. Then they write the ticket number in chalk on your bike seat, and you can't get your bike back unless you hand them the magic ticket when you're leaving. The process is annoying if you're in a rush, but they're good boys to have in your corner if you're worried about the bike disappearing.

Once I pulled up in front of two sunglasses shops that were directly next to each other. I checked the prices in one and then moved over to the next one. When the sole of my shoe left his property, the owner of the first shop screamed at me to move my bike. I was now, technically, a customer of another shop that was three feet removed from his, and was required to move my bike three feet as well.

I tried to defuse him with a wave and smile that said: it's all good, I'll just be a second. But it wasn't all good. He came out to the sidewalk and moved my bike over, all three feet, so it was now in front of the other shop.

If you're in a car, don't stress about finding a legal parking spot on the streets. I'd explain the rules of parking your car out on the streets, but there aren't any.

Auto drivers, particularly cabbies, have granted themselves carte blanche when it comes to parking. Little thought is given to cutting off circulation through an alley or side street just so the driver can duck into a store. It's supremely annoying, since the roads aren't wide enough for them to do that. It's also illegal, but the cops are never around to wave them on.

and a few passport photos. If you're in Hanoi, go to the Centre for Automotive Training and Mechanism, housed at 83a Ly Thurong Kiet Street. And in Saigon, the Office of Transportation can help you. They're at 63 Ly Tu Trong Street in District 1.

You should have the licence within a week, and depending on your visa or residency paperwork it can be valid for up three years. Technically, you're supposed to carry your domestic licence (or at least a copy of it) with your IDP. And once you have an IDP, it's pretty easy to get vehicle and accident insurance.

Just like visa rules, the process of getting a licence could always change. The Australian embassy has updated info for foreigners (pertinent for non-Aussies, too) on their website (http://vietnam.embassy.gov.au/hnoi/driving_in_vietnam.html).

The Gray Area

Now that the procedure's been outlined, let me tell you the truth about getting a licence: if you're a tourist (as I technically am) you don't need necessarily need one. Again, cash is king. One of your foreign privileges means you may not need to show a licence to rent a bike.

Of course, you ride at your own risk. If you're an unlicensed driver found at fault in a traffic accident—and you should expect that the dice won't roll the way of a foreigner if it boils down to a he-said/she-said situation—then jail time and severe financial penalties are not out of the question.

What if you get pulled over?

The police are allowed by law to confiscate your bike for up to 90 days if you don't have the necessary documentation.

Why would the cops pull you over? Well, keep reading.

Paying the Toll

In addition to dodging buses on the city roads, you also have to worry about what's happening on the sidelines. In Hanoi and Saigon, it's common to see checkpoints set up by traffic police. There's no end to the possible scenarios that could play out if you get pulled over, but here's a basic rundown:

Traffic checkpoints are set up along urban roads (and also on the highways). You'll see the police standing in knots on the sidewalk, with a web of traffic tape strung up around some cones. The police themselves wear mustard-coloured shirts (the locals call them "yellow fish").

If you're targeted by one, he'll stride out and block your path. If you try to swerve around them, they might hit you in the chest with the white batons they carry. Then they'll guide you to the roadside and pull your keys out of the ignition.

At that point, you'll have to show them your licence, and then be charged with your infraction either verbally or via a written ticket. Said infraction could be riding without a helmet, riding in the left-hand lane instead of the right or even the maddeningly vague "driving dangerously" (you could be charged with this even if you were actually driving quite nicely). Then you're expected to pay an on-the-spot fine. First-hand reports tell us that the police commonly expect 500,000 VND (approx. US$22) or more. If they pull you over without a licence, they're more likely to be interested in the immediate collection of the money rather than the hassle of trucking your bike away to the police station.

If you're pulled over, depending on the mood, and the language skills, of the cop, you might be able to negotiate the amount down a little. (But that's not a certainty.)

If you claim that you don't have the demanded amount money on you, the police have been known to escort "offenders" to a nearby ATM to withdraw cash. A friend of mine was pulled over on a highway outside of Saigon and was asked to pay US$500. He but didn't have that much money on him, so the police officer took him to an ATM.

Or the police might simply confiscate your licence and bike. You'll have to visit the police station where you'll have to fill out a form and pay a fee to reclaim everything. One way or another, you'll have to pay up.

When it Rains...

Besides the twin evils of traffic and checkpoints, you've got the rain to worry about. Storms frequently roll in from the South China Sea and lash the cities. And to me, it seems personal — they seem to only hit when I'm driving somewhere. Never before, never after, but exactly while I'm on the road.

You'll know when the downpour is coming because the Vietnamese motorists will sense it and, as one body, perform a choreographed pit stop. They'll pull their bikes to the shoulder and switch them off, which is a strange thing to actually witness. Because that's when a deep, eerie quiet will settle over the streets, and you'll realize that you've never heard Vietnam before without the overlaid soundtrack of a million buzzing engines.

Then the locals will remove ponchos from their scooter compartments, slide them on, and get back underway. They can perform this entire ritual before the first heavy drops hit.

And then your day got real bad, real fast. The gutters will overflow and bikes will bash into each other as bald tires glide over the wet road as if it's been slathered with Vaseline. And the poncho, while a relative miracle, has its flaws. Rainwater can leak in through your neck and soak the front of your shirt. And since your feet are more exposed due to the poncho's flappy, loose cut, your shoes will be soggy by the time you reach shelter.

Funny thing about shelter — the storm usually lets up as soon as you reach it. Or maybe it's just me. On days where the forecast calls for rain (so pretty much half the year) I put dry socks and a work shirt in my bag. The rain is a punishment for the cheap, unencumbered lifestyle expats have set up for themselves here. You can't have everything, after all.

You can get a poncho for about 30,000 VND in almost any mom-and-pop store. (And maybe some ridiculous sum like 300,000 VND if you're frantically trying to purchase one mid-storm — supply and demand!)

"What About Me?" Asks the Foreigner

Here's what you really need to know: I've only heard a few cases of foreigners being stopped. Our best hypothesis for this is that the traffic cops, uncomfortable with performing a shakedown in English, simply let us pass through the gauntlet. I drove past a checkpoint one day sans helmet, since mine had been stolen that morning, and wasn't stopped. Expats exist in an odd loophole. We can't expect it to stay open forever, but this is how it works for now.

But it does happen. If you are pulled over, just play dumb and hand them a little cash if they ask for it.

STAYING SAFE

At this point in the book you already know you've got to stay sharp and keep your head on a swivel if you want to survive traffic, or even a walk across the street. Outside of traffic, there are still a few things to be cognizant of.

Between Hanoi and Saigon, Saigon is generally regarded as wilder. There are more than a few "bag snatch" stories circulating — that's a manoeuvre performed by thieves who dart by you on a motorbike and grab your purse or shoulder bag (or your phone or camera). However, I've never met anyone in Hanoi who's encountered this. My helmet was once stolen off my bike handlebars, but that's the closest brush I've had with the criminal underworld. On a global scale, Vietnam is comparatively much safer than the stories would suggest.

Now, wherever you are, anything can happen, and there're always creeps. Three young women I know were driving up a dirt road in the woods outside Hanoi when a local man blocked their path on his motorbike. He approached and groped one of them before they were able to push past him and rode away. Similar situations have been reported

Safety Tips

All right, I know you're an adult, so forgive me for lecturing. But I must recommend the obvious precautions, no matter where in Vietnam you wind up:

- Keep an eye or two on your bag when Facebooking in the café.
- If you're of means (and as a Westerner in Vietnam, you probably are), be inconspicuous about it.
- Resist the urge to take long, winding walks through the city's more underdeveloped areas after midnight.
- A money belt is a good idea while you're scrambling through chaos in the markets and pinballing off everyone else in the crowd.
- After parking your motorbike or scooter, double-check that you've locked the handlebars (they'll show you how to do it if you rent one). Also, ask the owner (if you're renting one) for a chain lock that you can feed through the wheel spokes, so no one can roll the bike away while you're gone. Bike theft isn't overwhelmingly common, but it does happen.
- Keep your temper dialed down. It's a statistical certainty that you'll get ripped off by a taxi driver or a vendor, and it's even more certain that they'll play dumb if you confront them. That'll get you steamed, but don't start swinging — the police probably won't be inclined to side with your account of things.

since then, in the darkened avenues bracketing the nightlife hotspots. Another friend, a young British guy, was mugged while walking home one evening and had his phone stolen.

While these outliers tar the country's reputation, other outliers counterbalance them in turn. On a bike trip, two friends of mine dropped their backpack — with their passports and cash in it — on the shoulder of the highway. They had just resigned themselves to the loss and the imminent headache of passport replacement when they got a call. A Vietnamese family had picked up their bag, found their contact information inside and gotten in touch with them.

HEALTH AND HOSPITALS

Vietnamese healthcare is Exhibit A of "You get what you pay for."

Public hospitals are affordable, but that's probably the last good thing you can say about them. If you visit one you should steel yourself for the possibility of very long wait times. Vietnamese hospitals can be dank, bleak places that reek of cigarette smoke and are stocked with substandard medical equipment that look like film props from a period piece.

The staff is another matter — it's more likely than not that they won't speak English on the level you'll want them to (well, it is their country). But beyond that, it's arguable that the impetus to provide thorough, quality care just isn't there.

The occupation of doctor used to be a respected one in Vietnam, but its status has slipped in recent times. Those who work in the public hospitals don't pull down a great income (somewhere within US$250–400 a month.) Doctors have tried to close the wage gap by accepting bribes from patients in exchange for preferential treatment, and they've been caught on numerous occasions. Malpractice and incompetence (due to any number of factors, including an overload of patients) are also recurring issues. They've been repeatedly reported to the Ministry of Health, provoking several still-ongoing investigations in response.

I can't wholeheartedly recommend a public hospital here. But take heart — there's another way.

Private Clinics

You can find private clinics here that cater to foreign patients, and the doctors there will probably speak English.

It won't be too hard to find one online, and a few are listed in the Resource Guide on page 238. I'd check over the phone or online to see if they accept your insurance.

If you don't have insurance, then this cheap dreamland you live in all of a sudden goes away, reality sets back in, and you're all of a sudden paying premium prices again. I once had a heat rash on my leg and went to get it checked out. I was charged US$80 at a clinic to see an English-speaking doctor, and another US$20 for a prescription. Those prices probably trend a bit higher than normal, but at least now you have some ballpark figures.

The takeaway: Vietnam is cheap — until you get sick.

Insurance

It's a very, very good idea to get covered. It's worth it for the motorbikes alone, being that you'll spend a portion of your day either straddling one of these death rockets, or walking around in the way of them. Coverage here works like you're probably used to: Rates depend on your age and health.

If you're not getting insurance through your job in Vietnam, then see if your policy back home covers your trip.

But you might be here as a traveller — and that's OK. There is, of course, an industry devoted to covering all the vagabonds out there. It's easy to check out a reputable provider such as Travelex or Allianz (and those are just two of many) online and get a quote to see how much it'll be to stay covered during your trip.

Traveller's insurance can help you out if you're just passing through Vietnam. If you're staying for a few months, you can also check out Blue Cross Vietnam or Baoviet, which is the largest insurance company in Vietnam. Be sure to ask the full battery of questions, and make sure you're getting covered for any procedures you need, and that your plan will let you seek treatment at private clinics (if that's what you want).

Pharmacies

Any major intersection in the big cities probably has one or two pharmacies within eyesight.

The prices are low and the selection of over-the-counter ailments is decent. I went to the pharmacy a few times back before I knew any Vietnamese, and I usually looked up the medicine's actual name (not the brand name) beforehand so I could show it to the staff. They probably won't speak amazing English, but every pharmacist I've talked with so far has been able to walk me through the dosage schedule of whatever they're giving me. The more helpful ones will write it down for you.

Check the expiration dates on the medicine before you take it home. Pharmacies here have been busted for selling out-of-date (or counterfeit) meds before. But for what it's worth, I'm not too concerned. I've guinea-pigged my way through a handful of pharmacy trips here, and I'm still alive.

You'll just have to abide by what should be Vietnam's unofficial motto: You never know.

Dentists

I've ridden with a few taxi drivers, middle-aged working men who had charcoal-black smiles and breath that could kill flowers. With all the American dental propaganda drilled into me as a schoolkid, I'd forgotten that seeing a dentist is a relative luxury.

When it's time to see the dentist (if you're like me, that time came and went a few months ago), you probably won't even need Google to find one. In the square-mile around my place in Hanoi, there's maybe six dental clinics, and those are just the ones I've noticed.

Apprehension is normal, but you'll be all right. The staff should be helpful and the equipment, clean. Go with your gut, and if the place doesn't seem up to par, just politely leave.

Count on routine procedures being affordable, especially if they're compatible with your insurance. Price quotes are low enough that dental tourism is a thing here. Clinics here will put up banners advertising how far foreign patients have flown to receive implants or root canals (a guy from Florida apparently had some work done at the dentist in my shopping centre). The intercontinental trip was apparently deemed a sound investment, even with airfare and visa costs added in.

Emergencies and Travel

Remember what I said about traffic? It slows everyone down, including ambulances. Once I was stuck in gridlock, absolutely unable to move, with an ambulance sitting right on my back wheel, siren wailing away. All I could do was offer up a few positive vibes for whatever unlucky soul was awaiting it.

Or maybe the ambulance drivers were just trying to bust out of traffic?

A few weeks later I was driving home from a friend's house and found a Vietnamese man unconscious on the road, with blood forming a puddle around his head. I didn't see a crashed bike nearby, so I figured he'd been the victim of a hit-and-run. Two passers-by called an ambulance, and I stuck around, thinking its arrival was imminent. It was midnight, after all, and there was no traffic to choke off movement through the city.

It took 30 minutes to arrive.

The takeaway: If you're in need of a fast lift to the hospital, a taxi is actually your best option (if you're in the position to hail one or get someone to hail it for you). There's far more likely to be one of them nearby than there is an ambulance.

On a motorbike trip in a countryside village? I'm not a betting man but if I were, I wouldn't plan on there being a pharmacy or clinic being right around the corner. Be careful, and remember that having a small first-aid kit in your bag never hurt anyone.

SCHOOLS

Stereotypes of Asian education hold true here, too: Vietnamese students are expected to wake up, put their heads in a book and keep them there. Families who have the means will load up their children's schedules with after-hours courses. Whether they're public or private school students, schoolchildren are almost unfailingly found in uniform. The school year runs in accordance with the September–June Western schedule. A six-day school week is common.

While school attendance is ostensibly mandatory in Vietnam, a birth certificate is required to enrol in school. As there is still an impoverished segment of the population who couldn't afford the trip to the delivery room, a number of children will grow up without the chance to be educated.

Tuition is supposed to be free until middle school. But primary schools, lacking proper funding, close the gap by charging superlative fees for everything from maintenance costs to pencils and paper. It's quite easy for disadvantaged local families to fall behind on these charges. The rub is that children, even if they have a birth certificate, aren't permitted to attend school if their parents can't pay up, a policy that's resulted in the exclusion of a percentage of have-nots. It's a somewhat curious twist of events for what's touted as a socialist state.

These will only be a concern if you plan on sending your children on a deep dive into local culture by enrolling them in a Vietnamese public school. But unless they're fluent in the language, which is pretty unlikely, going public would be a form of psychological torture for them. And this is to say nothing of the dry, rote educational methodology utilized here, which may be the schoolhouse equivalent of a Bataan Death March for any student who's thus far come up in a Western classroom.

Then there are private schools, which are wholly Vietnamese while at the same employing more variance in their curricula and instructional styles.

A schoolboy getting into his uniform for the day.
(Photo credit: Kevin Abery)

Going even further up the price ladder, we arrive at international schools. While they're the most expensive option, they're a much kinder bet for your student.

Turn to the Resource Guide on page 238 to see a list of international schools in both Hanoi and Saigon. Many of them accept applications year-round, and shopping around for the best fit should be easy as you're settling into your new city. I'd get on it as soon as possible, though. The better schools are magnets that pull in applicants so quickly that

Documents for School Admission

Here are a few of the documents to have on hand as you start to wade through the application process:

- Applicant's (your child's) birth certificate,
- Pertinent passports (yours and your child's),
- Work permit, employment contract or residency card of at least one parent,
- Applicant's standardized test results and school transcripts,
- Applicant's medical records, with vaccination certificates.

you might never get off the waiting list. You can probably also count on an interview or two (and the payment of application and admission fees) before Junior arrives for his first day of class.

BANKING

HSBC, ANZ, Standard Chartered and Citibank all maintain a presence here, which will give you one less headache upon arrival if you've already got an account with them.

On the Vietnamese side of things, Vietcom Bank, Sacombank and Asia Commercial Bank come recommended. Even on a tourist visa, many banks still let you open an account if you can show them an employment contract (to prove you're making money here legally) and have a housing lease to prove you're renting a place.

To open an account, go into a bank branch with these:
- Passport (with visa),
- Residence card (if applicable),
- Employment contract,
- Proof of address,
- Cash in VND so you can make an initial deposit on the spot, if requested. Most banks will ask for 3,000,000–6,000,000 VND.

Just know that, depending on the bank, foreign account holders might have to play by different rules when it comes to daily deposit, remittance and withdrawal limits.

On the Go

Once you've been issued a debit card you can begin looting the ATMs. There are plenty, don't worry—at least in the cities. In the countryside, all bets are off. But anyway, most ATMs have a 2,000,000 VND daily withdrawal limit (only about US$95). I've discovered that ANZ Bank, though, allows up to 5,000,000 VND.

Oh, and FYI: They're wise to fees over here. Be ready to pay up for international transfers, foreign ATM fees, early account closure and pretty much any transaction you make. Every time I make a withdrawal using my American debit card, I lose about US$11 due to the "convenience fees" levied.

It's usually faster to pay for purchases with cash, in Hanoi at least. Credit card machines have been in hotels and first-world (read: non-hole in the wall) restaurants for a little while now, and they've just made their way into import stores and chain coffee houses. But the thing is, they're pretty slow, and they take a coon's age to fetch the bank data and then finally spit out the receipt. A lot of people gum up the store lines — and everyone else's days — by throwing down plastic instead of cash.

TAXES

You love filing your taxes, right? Good, because you get to do them in Vietnam, too!

The Vietnamese have laid out different tax brackets for tax residents and non-tax residents. Right now, a tax resident is defined as anyone with a permanent or leased residence in Vietnam. If you're leasing, and your lease lasts 183 days or more, then you're a tax resident.

If you reside in Vietnam for an aggregate total of 183 days or more within a one-year period, you're a tax resident, too. A non-tax resident is someone who's in-country for less time than that. If that's you, you're charged a flat PIT (Personal Income Tax) rate of 20% on your earnings.

There's a sliding scale for tax residents. If you make

5 million VND or less per month, then the maximum you'll be charged on your income is 5%. The maximum tax rate is currently 35%. Vietnam has 10 income categories (wages, royalties, capital investments, just to name a few), and whichever of them your cash is coming from could also influence your rate. For a more detailed look at this, go to: www.vietnam-briefing.com/news/introduction-personal-income-tax-vietnam.html

For non-tax residents, your employer is supposed to register you as a foreigner worker and deduct your PIT for you, so you won't have to undergo the painful experience of forking over cash yourself.

And just so you don't end up as an international fugitive, do a little Googling or talk to your accountant to figure out whether your home government requires you to submit a tax return to them, too. I say this because, as an American, I have a nosy uncle who's very interested in how much cash I'm making in some dusty alley in the Orient.

CHAPTER 6

FOOD

❝ Ask not what you can do for your country.
Ask what's for lunch. **❞**

— Orson Welles, actor and director

IT ALL STARTS WITH PHO

The ubiquitous *pho* with extra noodles on the side.

I was teaching some of my students in an English class how to describe foods or items that an area is famous for. To do this, I modelled this sentence structure for them: "(Place) is known for its (thing)."

"How about Vietnam?" I asked. "Fill in the blank. Vietnam is known for its…"

Without second-guessing or hesitating, they all shouted, "*Pho.*"

Pho is both staple and king here. Vietnamese eateries back in the West serve it, so you might have had some before. But if you're still uninitiated, it's not pronounced how it looks. "*Pho*" doesn't rhyme with "no", but instead with "huh". (We'll have more fun with Vietnamese's counter-intuitive pronunciation in Chapter 8).

The basic recipe calls for a bowl of *banh pho* rice noodles and meat (probably chicken or beef), floating in broth. It's really as simple as it gets. The Vietnamese will eat it for every meal.

What you'll do is attack the long noodles by curling them around your chopsticks, and then scoop up the broth with a little flattened metal spoon. The nation's relaxed anarchy extends to its dining etiquette, so putting the bowl to your mouth and slurping loudly is acceptable.

Having been raised by a mother who had a militant obsession with table manners, the slurping noises do drive me insane, but that's something I'm working out with a therapist.

THE LOCAL FAVOURITES

Most Vietnamese restaurants have giant menus out front, so you'll know straight away whether they have what you're looking for.

But most restaurant menus also aren't written in English, and a lot of them don't have pictures. Back in the more reckless phase of my immersion, I just took to pointing to a random word on the menu, nodding to the server in the affirmative, then eating whatever they brought out to me. And what's surprised me about this aimless shotgunning method is that I've haven't been disappointed yet.

A friend of mine recently had a disastrous dinner, though. He pointed at a saucy dish on the menu and it ended being *tiet canh*, which is raw goose blood soup. He said that it tasted as good as it sounds.

Here are my personal food recommendations, compiled after a few months of recon:

Bun cha ("boon chah"): This dish is comprised of little grilled pork patties and white rice noodles, served with some vegetables and a special dipping sauce made of fish sauce mixed with sliced vegetables.

Former US President Obama visited Hanoi in 2016 and went to a *bun cha* place with celebrity chef Anthony Bourdain. Photos of their meet-up trended on social media for a day or so. (Later that year, I saw a silk painting of one of these photos for sale in an art gallery in Saigon.)

A few weeks after Obama's visit, I was in a new part of town and randomly chose a restaurant with *bun cha* listed on the sign out front. I got a subtle jolt of familiarity as I walked in, and then it hit me; it was the same spot where Obama had eaten. They'd put up poster-sized photos on all the walls of the president with his meal. There's actually a "Combo Obama" on the menu: *bun cha* served with a cold bottle of Bia Hanoi. (FYI, just in case you want the same experience, the restaurant is called Bun Cha Huong Lien and it's at 24 Le Van Huu in Hanoi's Hai Ba Trung District.)

The *bun cha* restaurant where former US president Obama took his famous meal.

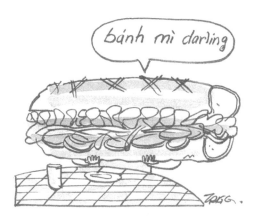

Bahn mi (pronounce the second word like "me"): Vietnam might have kicked the French out, but they kept their baguettes (*banh mi* is Vietnamese for "bread"). A *banh mi* sandwich is a baguette sliced open and filled with grilled pork belly or chicken, fried egg, or pâté, or cucumbers… you get the idea. Anything. Then they toast it for you.

It's a nice little fusion dish and could be your "gateway meal", if maybe you're in 'Nam against your volition and just can't get into the cuisine. In the busier areas, you can get *banh mi* at the little street stands on the corner. Just look for the towering baskets of baguettes. The *banh mi* vendors in Saigon have the market cornered on variety.

Pho chien gion ("phuh chee-en zahn"): Not as all-out ubiquitous as the previous items, but it's probably my favourite Viet dish. *Pho chien gion* is fried *pho* noodles that are cut and arrayed on the plate almost like pizza slices, then topped with bok choy or broccoli, along with fried beef. You pile everything on the fried noodles and dip it in soy sauce.

This one is worth tracking down. While you're digging in, you can almost feel the grease leaking into your bloodstream, but I think the flavour is worth any potential health consequences.

Other Dishes

One quick generalization: People who've travelled through both the top and bottom of the country will tell you that the food up in the North is saltier, and down South meals trend on the sweeter side.

Even if you only look at their soups, the Vietnamese have come up with a fairly eternal number of culinary permutations. (This is what happens in a culture that spent a few dozen generations grabbing whatever happened to be lying around and dropping it into a pot.) I can't list everything on the menu, but here's a fast glance at some options.

- **Banh cuon:** Translucent spring rolls (made of steamed rice cake) filled with pork or shrimp and greens. Sometimes sprinkled with bits of fried onion.
- **Banh khot:** Bite-sized rice pancakes topped with herbs, vegetables and shrimp.
- **Banh trang tron:** A spicy snack of torn-up rice paper mixed with herbs, squid, quail eggs, and other seafood.

Women cooking *banh cuon* in an eatery.

- **Banh xeo:** A fried pancake stuffed with (again) pork or shrimp, with some vegetables to balance it all out.
- **Bo kho:** Vietnamese beef and vegetable stew.
- **Bat chien:** Fried rice cakes topped with green onions and eggs.
- **Bun bo hue:** A rice noodle soup made with beef, noted for its lemongrass flavour.
- **Bun rieu:** (Another) rice noodle soup, with tofu and seafood floating in the broth.
- **Bun thit nuong:** Not a soup! A cousin of *bun cha*, this dish gives you herbs, pork and egg rolled mixed into a bowl of rice vermicelli noodles.
- **Ca kho to:** Braised catfish, cut up and seasoned before it's served.
- **Cha ca:** A seafood dish of sautéed fish, onions, and rice noodles.
- **Com binh dan:** A category of rice meals usually served with either pork, fish or tofu.
- **Com tam suon nuong:** Broken rice (very prevalent in the South), served with grilled pork.
- **Goi cuon:** Spring rolls made of rice paper wrapped around seafood and vermicelli noodles.
- **Hu tieu nam vang:** (Yet another) noodle soup, built around pork and shrimp.
- **Thit bo nuong la lot:** Beef, seasoned and wrapped up in betel leaves.

Meals on Wheels

Look out for the little carts that appear on the roadside concurrent with rush hour. *Banh mi*, *pho*, kebabs and almost anything else are prepared in little micro-kitchens (pans, gas flames — the whole deal). The vendors cook quickly, and you

A street food vendor serving *banh mi* sandwiches in Hanoi.

A vendor serves some hot noodles on the sidewalk in Danang.

rarely spend more than 30,000 VND for a bite. It's only on your second or third look that you'll notice these little kitchens are actually... motorbikes.

Vendors have constructed vehicular Frankensteins by attaching a sidecar-like structure to their bike frames and then piling stoves and meat racks on top of it. They bolt and screw the whole precarious arrangement together, and then fire up the bike engine and find a corner upon which to set up shop.

Take note: Some of them will hustle you. I was hanging out with another tourist in Saigon who ordered two *banh mi* at 15,000 VND apiece. He paid with a 100,000 VND bill, and was owed back 70,000. The vendor gave him 20,000 VND.

"You still owe me 50,000 dong," said the tourist.

"I have no more money," the vendor said.

And then he drove off.

RESTAURANTS

They're everywhere. Just drive up on the sidewalk and park wherever the staff signals is OK. Busier restaurants might valet your bike away for you.

A lot of Vietnamese joints will be holes in the wall. Inside, everyone will crammed up close to the aluminium tables, their shouts bouncing off the ceramic tiles. Take your cues from the other diners. Eat quickly, chew with your mouth open, drop your gristle and napkins on the floor—whatever you want. It'll be a feeding frenzy, and in the rush and the madness, anything goes.

Vietnamese zoning laws seem to be pretty lax; I haven't seen much of a delineation between residential and commercial real estate. Once, I was waiting to use the restroom in the back of a small restaurant. It was taking a while, but I could hear someone moving around in there, so I decided to wait instead of wandering around on the street to find another restroom. I ended up having a stand-off with the locked door for about 15 minutes.

A woman eventually came out, with a towel wrapped

Dining Etiquette

When you're eating with people you know, or at someone's home, here are some guidelines to make it seem like you've done your homework.

- In a restaurant, summon a server by calling out *ban oi*. That sort of translates out to "hey, friend, come here."
- Wipe off your utensils with a napkin before you use them (you'll see why in the next section). If the chopsticks are wooden, rub them together a few times to scrape off any splinters.
- When you pass a dish to someone else, support it with both hands. It's polite, and the food won't spill.
- Don't eat your food straight from the communal serving dish. Transfer the food you want to your own bowl before you put it in your mouth.
- It's all right to pick up your bowl and hold it in one hand while you poke through your food with your chopsticks.
- Take a socialist approach to the meal. Try all the dishes on the table before zeroing in on one that you're really partial to. And even then, take it easy. This will let others get a chance to dig into it.
- By the same token, the meat is usually the most expensive part of the meal, so try to be conservative with it—even if it's achingly delicious.
- When you're full, announce this vocally, as sort of a casual aside, so that no one will try to offer you more food, provoking a rejection on your part (this might be seen as rude).
- When you're finished eating, put your chopsticks on top of your rice bowl, as if to close it off from further helpings. This is another signal that you're full.
- In a restaurant, just know that, in deference to the patriarchy, the men at the table might be served first.
- The institution of tipping doesn't exist here. You won't get bad service, but you might have to put in a little effort to get your server's attention. If you're eating in a busier restaurant, the only way to do so might be by firing off a flare gun. (FYI, a lot of restaurants have started factoring in a 10% service charge to the bill).
- Take your time, if you have it. Try not to dine and dash. A meal in Vietnam is a community ritual of fellowship and connection.

around her head. She'd been taking a shower. That restaurant was just a business enterprise her family had set up in their home's common area.

Don't Read This Before Lunch

Most restaurants on the street will give you stout wooden chopsticks that are "washed" after each meal before being re-deployed out to the dining area.

Now let's talk about why I put the word "wash" in scare quotes up there. My friend used to work as a beer promoter, and she visited about a dozen restaurants each night and got a look behind the curtain. She said that it's more common than not for workers in the kitchens to just spray down the dishes and chopsticks with cold water instead of scrubbing them with soap. Either that, or they'll drop the dish into a plastic bucket of brackish water with chunks of food floating in it, pull it out, dry it, and call it a day.

There's more — the ounce of beer that a moderate drinker may leave in his glass after a meal? It's poured back into a pitcher, where it mixes with the backwashed leftovers from a dozen other drinkers. The lukewarm mixture is cooled in the fridge, then poured back out into your glass when you arrive at the restaurant and order a beer.

Vietnam does have a Ministry of Health, but it's safe to say that restaurant owners aren't quaking in their boots, wondering when they'll be inspected.

It's best to think of any food poisoning as a rite of passage and a chance to build up antibodies that will serve you well for the rest of your time here. Only twice so far have I been hit with honest-to-God food poisoning. But considering the bacteria and supergerms my immune system have been up against here in Vietnam, I think that's a pretty decent record.

'Nam's Finest

You'll do your time at the dirty tables, and save a few buckets of money as you do—which should make it easy to justify enjoying the work of a trained chef. Vietnam's refined dining is as varied as you'd expect from this cultural kaleidoscope of a country.

Here are some gourmet establishments that come recommended:

Hanoi

- **Quan An Ngon**: Traditional *kiem pho* and *ngam nu pho*, *banh cuon*, grilled squid, hotpot. Has multiple locations in Hanoi.
- **La Verticale Hanoi**: Duck terrine, tuna with lemongrass, Enoki mushrooms with blue river prawn and Coriander. A French place, so look forward to a good wine pairing.
- **Pots 'n Pans**: *Bun chay* rice noodle soup, spring rolls stuffed with vegetables and herbs, lotus seed and perfume mushroom soup.
- **The Hanoi Social Club**: Western breakfast, gourmet salads, burgers and sandwiches. It's also a performing arts venue.

Saigon

- **Dong Pho Restaurant**: *Bun bo hue* soup, salmon soup, chicken in olive sauce—and they have French salads and seafood on offer as well.
- **Com Nieu Sai Gon**: Dumplings, *bong lau* fish soup, *com dap* smashed rice. This is a spot recommended by Anthony Bourdain.
- **Nha Hang Ngon Restaurant**: Grilled crab, spring rolls, *banh khot* shrimp cakes and lots of *pho*. The

restaurant is set up in an old French villa.

- **La Villa French Restaurant**: French wine, *foie gras*, pan-fried duck breast, roasted pork.

> If you're sharing plates with others, you might end up with some leftovers. To have the restaurant staff box it up for you, say: *"Mang di nhe (mong dee nay)!"*

SPECIAL DIETS

Vegetarians and Vegans

What constitutes as "meat" seems to, amusingly, still be a matter of debate in this country. Some vegetarian friends who've been hosted for dinner by Vietnamese families have politely mentioned that they don't eat meat, but would be glad to try anything else — and have been served fish anyway.

But thanks to the primacy of Buddhism in Viet culture, it's not hard to find vegetarian (*chay*) meals in Vietnam. Here are the magic words to tell a restaurant server that you're a vegetarian: "*Toi an chay* (toy ahn chay)." To ask for a dish in a restaurant without meat, say "*khong thit*" — it literally means "no meat".

Go out with a local friend if you can, because they can speak to the servers for you and find out what's safe to order (some dishes are prepared with a meat or fish-based broth).

Halal Food

The search for Halal food in the country and in the smaller urbanities will likely be a fruitless one. But in the big cities, anything is possible; international grocery stores should have serviceable selections of halal food and snacks. The Halal Certification Agency of Vietnam (http://halal.vn — select "English" at the top right below the header) has indicated the products that are safe to buy with a stamp. If you want to dine out, check out these webapges:

- (Hanoi) www.hanoimuslimtours.com/Travel-Guide/halal-restaurants-hanoi
- (Hanoi) www.holidayssg.com/muslim-food-guide-in-hanoi-2/
- (Saigon) www.havehalalwilltravel.com/blog/10-halal-restaurants-in-ho-chi-minh-for-your-gastronomic-adventure/

Food Allergies

Here's how to say you're allergic to nuts:

- *"Dung cho nuts, toi khong an duoc."*
  (No nuts, please. I'm allergic.)

For other allergies, replace the word "nuts" with:

- *Sua* (dairy),
- *Do bien* (seafood).

If you're daunted by how to pronounce those (I can relate) then write the phrases down so you can show them to the restaurant staff. Hang tight, because we'll talk more about pronunciation in Chapter 8.

WHEN THE CLOCK STRIKES FIVE

Since it's rare that I encounter a teetotalling traveller, I figure that this section will be of some use to you. Finding an evening beer in the city is going to be the easiest search of your life.

Between the Western-style bars and the Viet joints, there are so many magic-hour drinking spots that you'll never be able to hit them all, even if you convert to Buddhism while here and earn another pass at life.

Since you know what a Western bar is like, let's talk about the Vietnamese places. Here's a broad-strokes outline of the street beer you can find...

...In the North

Those based in Hanoi and its environs get down with some *bia hoi*. "*Bia*" is, as you maybe guessed, the Vietnamese dropped-r pronunciation of "beer", and "*hoi*" translates to "air" or "gas".

Bia hoi is both the name of the beer and the location where it's consumed. For example: "Let's head to the *bia hoi* for some *bia hoi*" is a statement that makes perfect sense.

The beer itself is locally-brewed each morning and shipped out to *bia hoi* by barrel. Being "air beer," it's a featherweight brew (think Bud Lite). Most batches register somewhere in the neighbourhood of a 3% alcohol content. A light jab to the liver, nothing more.

I find a *bia hoi* jaunt to be a soothing, guiltless evening power-down ritual. The *hoi* are overlit, tend to hover somewhere near capacity, and quiver with ambient joy as the collective stress of the crowd dissipates. The Vietnamese like their beer, and they like to have many rounds of it. But my unscientific takeaway from Vietnamese drinking here is that they seem to moderate a bit better than their neighbours in the northeast (I've seen blacked-out salarymen lying facedown on the benches and sidewalks of Seoul, Beijing, and Tokyo—but in Vietnam the heathens are more elusive). They'll get friendly enough to soldier up and say hello, but won't get too sloppy.

Most *hoi* servers I've had have been

sharp on the lookout and usually reload your glass before you even have a chance to ask them. And most *hoi* also serve food. There's not a huge amount of consistency among all these establishments, but you'll probably find some of the following. If you're into eating a veritable zoo's worth of animals, well, the *hoi* has you covered:

- **Lau** (hot pot): Any mix of vegetables, eggs, meat and seafood, cooked up as a soup in a communal pot on the table. A popular Vietnamese dinner in general.
- **Com rang dua bo**: Fried rice and beef.
- **Ga hap la chanh**: steamed chicken with lemon leaves, and **ga rang muoi**: pan-fried chicken with salt. Those are just two of many chicken dishes.
- **Mi xao bo**: Fried wheat noodles with beef.
- **Bo xao cai xanh**: Stir-fried beef and bok choy.
- **Trau xao la lot**: Stir-fried buffalo wrapped in green leaves.
- **Ech xao mang**: Stir-fried frog with bamboo.

Just go by the photos, and pick what looks good.

You Can't Afford Not to Drink it

Why haven't I been home in so long? my American friends ask. Well, because over here I can get a buzz for about a dollar. My choice *bia hoi*, on Ma May street in Hanoi's Old Quarter, charges 5,000 VND (about US$0.20) a glass.

Be forewarned: Some markets don't have cold beer. They'll bring you a warm bottle and a plastic cup of ice. You pour the beer into the cup, and try to drink it down before the ice melts and waters down your brew.

...And Down South

I walked all over Saigon and only spotted a few *bia hoi* and

The North's Cinderella Laws

Vietnam's exotic joys and liberties, the very same enticements that inspire short-term tourists to become expats proper, are balanced out by a nightly annoyance: Vietnam has an unofficial 12am bedtime—though I've noticed that it's only religiously enforced in the North.

If you're still having a few out at a streetside *hoi* when the clock strikes 12, a few men in baggy green shirts will roll up in a truck, draw their batons, and send you packing. Basically: You're allowed to be out of your house, but you can't be in a bar, because those are all technically supposed to close at midnight.

The concept was best stated by the band Semisonic in their immortal hit "Closing Time"—"You don't have to go home/but you can't stay here."

This is something of a curious method, because while Vietnam craves the tourist dollar, they also simultaneously deny it to themselves by cutting off the cash flow every night. There are rumours afloat that the government is starting to ease up on their draconian control, but as of this writing (December 2016), the cops were still prowling the city on nightly shutdown duty.

If you're booted off your perch by the 5-0, there will still be somewhere else to crawl to. Some places remain brazenly, proudly open until 2am or 3am, with speakers pumping and floodlights sweeping the sky. But those won't be your only options—do a little due diligence and make the right connections, and you'll figure out where the quieter speakeasy spots are.

Going to the speakeasies feels straight-up clandestine. In a beat out of spy thriller, you roll over to one of them, rap on the steel security curtain, and someone inside will roll it up to waist-height to let you in. You'll duck under it and have another drink inside, the buzz amplified by the thrill that you're "on the run" from the cops. You rebel!

Saigon, in deference to its vibrant, open image, keeps entire streets open.

Exhibit A: District 1's Bui Vien Street—the "Street of Foreigners". That one keeps on rocking until 5am.

a few beer gardens with stashes of bottled beer.

The city has instead leaned into its grandfathered-in European heritage by putting up a bunch of Czech-style beer halls. I walked into one of them on Pasteur Street, which is one of the city's microbrewing hubs. Inside, I found wood-plank flooring, soaring rafters, servers in outfits that could double as Oktoberfest Halloween costumes, and brewing vats the size of asteroids.

Beer halls will have what you came for: Old World-style beers (descriptors like "stout", "black" and "blond" are a sight for sore eyes) on tap, served in those huge, heavy cut-glass mugs that you could knock out a rhino with.

Until you open the menu, there will be absolutely nothing in sight to signify that you're still in Vietnam.

COFFEE AND TEA

The French brought their coffee with them on their Far Eastern adventure, and now that they're gone, Vietnam's taken the bean and run with it. The country is, right now, the world's second-largest coffee exporter. Coffee is grown in fields in the Central Highlands and also in the southeastern provinces.

Vietnam's café culture has surged along with the country's coffee output. Café signage is usually small and unobtrusive — they don't have marketing-conscious corporate overlords to appease — you'll have to stop and focus for a second to realize how just many cafés have

Two friends spending a leisurely afternoon together over a few cuppa.

occupied any given city street. Then you'll realize how many options you have; you can throw a rock with your weak arm in any direction and it'll land in a coffee cup.

All these cafés are duelling over the same customer base — but nearly everyone stays in business. A long, languishing sit over a cup of coffee has become a fixture of Vietnamese social life, at least for those who have the time for long, languishing sits.

Perform your very own sit inside the café, if you want to be screened off from the street chaos. Or, if you're after the immersive experience, you can take one of the little wooden tables they've set up on the sidewalk, and watch the city churn around you. This is my top method for killing time while I wait for the bonfire of rush-hour traffic to burn itself out.

Cafés will almost always have hot tea, too. There's a lot of variance between the menus, but it's not too hard to chase down smoothies, or bubble tea.

Oh yeah, remember what I said about the cops crashing the party? That can happen at the cafés too, but at any time of day. The authorities may come pay a visit and reshuffle the furniture on the sidewalk. I was having coffee one morning and a truck of soldiers pulled up and made us all move inside the café, where we stood for a few awkward minutes, holding our hot cups, until they left.

Following the brief irritation, the café staff will usually just help you relocate back out to the sidewalk, where you may return to your previously-scheduled caffeination.

Vietnamese Coffee is…

…a strong brew that runs through a French drip filter and into your cup. When crunched into Vietnamese, the word coffee becomes *ca phe*. The standard *ca phe* presentation involves a layer of condensed milk resting undisturbed on the bottom of the glass, like sediment, and you stir it up into the coffee to neutralize its strong taste. Check the menu for *ca phe sua* (literally "coffee milk") or *ca phe nau* ("coffee brown")—both refer to black coffee mixed with milk.

Black-coffee bloke that I am, I'm used to a pure blast of caffeine. I was confident I could take my *ca phe* straight, sans milk. I ordered it as such—and as much as I wish that this story has a different ending—I couldn't drink it. Black Vietnamese *ca phe* is truly, deeply bitter and almost verges upon rancid.

Some menus will give you an option for fresh milk, if going condensed makes it too sweet for you. Can you get an iced coffee? Yes you can. It's called *ca phe da*. (With milk, it's called *ca phe sua da*).

Try an iced coffee variety called *bac xiu* (pronounced "bock sue"). It's iced coffee, but with a lot of condensed milk in it. If you see it on a menu, pull the trigger.

Smoking

Adjacent to a nice cup of coffee is the leisurely pastime of lighting one up.

In case you're being shamed for this habit back home in the West, take heart: smoking is still enduringly popular in this corner of Asia. I asked a few middle-aged Vietnamese men what their favourite hobby was, and they said, "Sitting on the street with a newspaper and a cigarette."

In what's surely the defining multitasking manoeuvre of the new millennium, you'll see people texting and smoking while also driving a motorbike. As I said before, try to get a helmet that protects your entire face, not just the top of your head. Once, the driver in front of me flicked his cigarette over his shoulder and it hit my visor, sending up a little spray of sparks.

In the markets up north, you can take a hit of Vietnamese tobacco (*thuoc lao*) from a bamboo pipe they'll have leaning against some of the tables. It's legal—and quite strong. Take a seat before you try it.

That's Nice. But What If I Hate Trying New Things?

It's actually pretty hard to find the archetypal cup of (Western-style) brewed coffee over here. For an unadulterated taste of the home country, you can hit up Starbucks or Coffee Bean & Tea Leaf.

Vietnam's answer to Starbucks is Highlands Coffee. They operate pleasant, chilly shops, with flatscreen TVs on the walls, but despite all the Western appropriations, they still don't serve a regular brewed coffee. Instead they have a hot Americano (if you don't speak café-Italian, that's a shot of espresso dropped in hot water). They do give out a complimentary dime-sized shortbread cookie with each order, so that's nice, I guess.

Down South, Phuc Long Coffee & Tea is a popular chain coffeehouse. They have an Americano, too. Locals dig it for the peach tea and milk tea.

Use your times in the little street cafés as branch-out opportunities. Playing mad scientist with more ingredients left behind by the French, the Vietnamese have created some drinks that sound ridiculous, but that you should order anyway. Try these:

- **Sua chua ca phe**: Yogurt in a glass, sometimes mixed with fruit, with a skim of coffee on top. Stir it in and go for it.
- **Ca phe trung**: Egg coffee. Sounds ridiculous, but again, just go for it. The flavours fuse together and end up suggesting more of a chocolatey taste than anything else.
- **Sinh to ca phe chuoi bo**: A smoothie where coffee's been blended in with avocado and banana.

FAST FOOD

Never fear, globalization is here. I've come across foreign outposts of Burger King, McDonald's, KFC, Pizza Hut, Domino's, Baskin Robbins, and Popeye's Chicken... there are more, but you get the idea. These are essentially culinary embassies, and they'll be a refuge for you, if you're jonesing for the chemicals laced into the combo meals. There's no shame in indulging; you might see me there.

Asia's now in the fast food game, too. Lotte is a brand you'll become aware of here. It's a Japanese/Korean conglomerate (headquartered in a skyscraper stabbed right into the centre of Hanoi) that's fielded their own fast food chain, Lotteria. Besides the classic burger-and-fries meals, check out the chicken baskets, chips, ice cream, and pork sandwiches.

DELIVERY

You remember the part about motorbikes, right? If the Vietnamese can load up a family of five and their pets and a chest of drawers on a motorbike all at the same time, then they can of course bring you a meal.

Most Western places deliver. What I usually do is pick up their business card and affix it to the fridge so I can give them a call when I'm feeling lazy, which is every day. (Even though I've travelled from another hemisphere to get here, leaving the block is often out of the question.)

Vietnamese restaurants deliver too, but you won't be able to gauge which places do and don't—and what their phone number is—until you visit them in person. If you're ordering from a local place by phone, you will probably need a Vietnamese collaborator to do the talking for you.

If you're after Western food, almost all of those restaurants have staff members who can speak enough English to settle up your order over the phone, in case your Vietnamese isn't there yet (and you are going to learn, right?) Make sure you double and triple-check your address with them over the phone. Usually the driver will give you a call if he or she gets lost, which is probably going to happen if you live in an alley. It'll make everyone's life easier if you leave your apartment and lean outside the building gate to wave the driver down.

There might be a small delivery fee, and while tipping isn't expected, I like to hook up the driver with an extra 5,000–10,000 VND as thanks, especially if it's a hot day.

Check out these sites for local food and grocery delivery in urban Vietnam:

- www.vietnammm.com (yes, that's three "m"s. The site also has a smartphone app.)
- eat.vn
- chop.vn

ENTERTAINING AT HOME

I've found that, most of the time, Vietnamese people lead with the invites: They'll ask you to join them at their homes or at a restaurant. But don't be afraid to invite them over to your spot. In my experience, Vietnamese friends haven't just stopped by the house for dinner—they've brought ingredients, showed us how to make spring rolls, and even helped with the dishes afterward. (As someone with an aversion to both cooking and cleaning, I think I'm in the right country). Evenings at home are more immersive events that give you more time to connect with your guests.

You can also prepare Western food for the evening, which is an invitation your friends won't reject. However, I have a hunch that they'll indulge in whatever you prepare primarily in the interest of being courteous and respecting your offer. I say this because many Vietnamese people I meet prefer their own cuisine to foreign offerings, and are keen to introduce you to as many of their dishes as you'll allow them to.

CHAPTER 7

ENJOYING THE CULTURE AND TRAVEL

> ❝Culture's worth huge, huge risks.
> Without culture we're all totalitarian beasts.❞

— Norman Mailer, writer

CULTURE AND THE ARTS

Modern Vietnamese culture is what you get when you take the livelihood and creativity of 54 ethnic groups, and then filter it all through a thousand years of Chinese influence. But that's only part of the process—you then split the resulting nation in two and add in arbitrary amounts of French, Portuguese, Cambodian and American cultural exports. Wait a few decades, then rejoin these two halves, step back and see what it all looks like.

Let me bullet-point a few Vietnamese cultural facets that you might want to take a closer look at—or that you might end up stumbling across in your sojourn anyway.

Music

Sure, Vietnamese produces pop music, but good luck differentiating it from K-pop or any of its other cousins.

Now, are you interested in hearing some traditional Vietnamese music?

Trick question. You're going to hear it whether you want to or not.

I'd need another book to outline this country's traditional music and the styles therein, what with all the provinces and ethnic groups who've been composing and playing for millennia. But since that's not the job, let's see if I can do it in a paragraph. Here goes:

A while back, northern Vietnam brought *ca tru*, a lute and

light percussion-backed genre of traditional music, to the table. This is just one sub-genre of the nation's music, but it's unmistakably and emblematically Vietnamese. In the 13th century, the North also birthed a folk music style called *quan ho*, which originated in Bac Ninh province near the Red River Delta. In 2009, *quan ho* was marked as an Intangible Cultural Heritage by the UNESCO. Now for the South. Broadly speaking, southern traditional songs may incorporate more guitars and violins. Larger orchestras that play Vietnamese music fiddle with (pun intended) any combination of traditional flutes and stringed instruments.

Now, with the title of this book in mind, let me explain how music plays into culture shock in Vietnam.

Drive far enough through a Vietnamese city and eventually you'll come across a lighted platform set up on the shoulder of the road. Performers will be standing behind the mic and belting out traditional songs to passing traffic (you'll find that usually these installations are charity performances). What do traditional songs sound like? There's a lot of whiny, jarring chord changes and what seems to be a compositional dependence on whole notes. And when it comes to the delivery there's a whole lot of closed-eyed wailing, as each song seems to reduce its singer to an emotional wreck.

There's also something about the volume. Even with headphones in, and travelling by on a motorcycle (with a helmet on), it seems to take a full minute to get out of the blast radius of the loudspeakers.

Now this is where I stick my dumb foreign head into

I asked a few classes of mine who the Vietnamese equivalent of the Beatles would be, and they named ballad composer Trinh Cong Son, who wrote music before, during and after the Vietnam War.

the middle of things. I've caught myself thinking that I love everything about Vietnam, except for the music. I'm all for pride in tradition, but personally, I don't get it. And I *shouldn't* get it; Vietnamese music evolved independently from every sonic influence I've ever encountered in the West. To my ear, the scales and chords and melodies are abrasive, cacophonous and arrhythmic. But to each their own, right? After all—a Vietnamese man would probably fling himself out with nosebleeds if he were ever in attendance at a Garth Brooks concert.

Before you deride my cultural insensitivity, keep in mind that it's not just me—some Vietnamese scammers literally use these songs as a weapon. Sometimes you'll be sitting at a *bia hoi* and a guy will station himself out front with a microphone and portable speaker. The thing about the speaker is that its volume knob has apparently been turned all the way to the right and snapped off.

The singer begins to work through a folk tune, quite loudly, as if he's the last man on Earth, howling to the heavens for attention. This will provoke shouts of annoyance and winces *en masse*, but outside of assault, there's no way to remove him. What'll happen is the boss of the *bia hoi* will run interference by hustling out and handing our Vietnamese Idol some money in exchange for an immediate eviction.

And then he heads down the street to burst more eardrums.

Calligraphy

Go deep enough into the street markets and you'll find scrolls inked with Vietnamese calligraphy (*thu phap*).

Before you page ahead, I should tell you that it's not exactly what you expect it to be. From a few strides away, the words

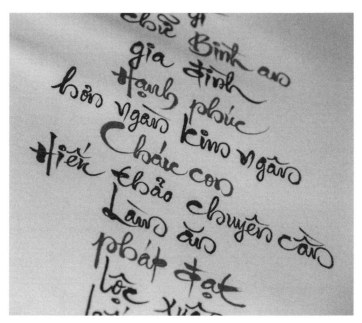
Vietnamese calligraphy is a fusion of Eastern and Western styles.

seem to masquerade as Mandarin Chinese characters. It's when you get closer that you realize that the writing is done with our own Roman alphabet (known here as the *quoc ngu*—more on that in Chapter 8.)

There are a few categories that I don't have the space to list, but what's worth mentioning is the foundational difference between Vietnamese and Western calligraphy. Rather than conveying information with a neat, practiced flourish, the emphasis in the Vietnamese method is on communicating emotion and feeling. So the overall effect is that the Vietnamese letters seem to shapeshift, contort and flow into each other, as if each design is a still frame pulled from an animated film.

Calligraphers channel the emotions that a certain word or phrase brings to mind, and reflect them in the scripts they produce. The works are completed with Chinese calligraphy brushes—not pens. Sometimes symbols or drawings are incorporated into the Vietnamese lettering.

I'm the furthest thing from an art collector, but a work of Vietnamese calligraphy is a purchase I think I could justify as a symbol of my stay here. It brings to mind how much seismic change and cultural fusion this land has witnessed. Their calligraphy is Eastern and Western, and also inflected with Chinese stylings—all while remaining Vietnamese.

I haven't been to one, but look around hard enough and you can find a live "performance", where calligraphers will inscribe their work on a banner in front of a crowd.

Silk Painting

Vietnamese silk painters learned European oil painting techniques during the colonization period, and incorporated what they found valuable into their own processes. The pre-World War II era is considered by some to be silk painting's "golden age".

During the production process, the silk is starched and stretched out by a frame, and then watercolours are applied. The colour of the silk canvas itself is commonly used at the background of the painting—the sky or the sea, for example. The texture of silk seems to have the binary power of both enlivening the colours used and also imbuing them with an otherworldly mystique.

Despite the lengthy, painstaking production process, silk paintings can be found in the markets or small galleries for somewhere in the neighbourhood of US$5–50.

Some of Vietnam's most famous silk paintings now hang in museums, but the fragility of silk is such that it won't be very long before they crack apart and decay.

Martial Arts

Korea has its taekwondo, Japan has its karate, and Vietnam has its Vovinam.

It's a full-contact martial art with armed and unarmed variations. After watching a few matches it seems that creativity is a huge component of Vovinam — the styles used and the variables involved likely verge upon infinite. Students learn scissor kicks, grapples, and how to scrap with and (defend themselves from) daggers, sticks, staffs and cutlasses. Even everyday objects like umbrellas make their way into the mix. So, a day at Vovinam practice is kind of like being in a Jackie Chan fight scene.

When you take the long view of history, then Vovinam is relatively new; it was developed in the 1930s, during the last act of French occupation. It's arguable that the art is a byproduct of the search for national pride (and also a form of protest) in the face of colonization. Vovinam's original moves and rhythms were developed by its founder, Nguyen Loc. Loc created the practice by taking traditional Vietnamese martial arts and then wedding them with influences from karate, taekwondo, and kung fu.

When he first fielded Vovinam in 1938, Nguyen said that he hoped it would contribute to the independence of Vietnam. This sounds a little strange when you remember that the 20th century was right in the middle of the gun age (what change were fisticuffs going to effect?), but maybe there was something to this; the French recognized Vovinam's militant potential, and banned it in 1942.

Modern practitioners wear a loose blue uniform called a *vophuc* (outside of the colour, it resembles its Japanese equivalent, the *karategi*). Coloured belts denote rank, with red being the highest level a student can reach.

The reasoning behind the belt colours is pretty cool — achieving the rank of yellow belt means you've only immersed yourself skin deep in the art, while possession of a red belt signifies that mastery of Vovinam has sunk into you to such an extent that it's now part of your blood. Only grandmasters may wear white, which means that Vovinam is now marrow deep within you.

The art, which was once imbued with political motivations, has shifted into one that focuses on discipline, as well as recognizing and overcoming the ego. Vovinam schools espouse a respectful mindset, and teach students to use their skills only in matters of self-defence or in the preservation of justice.

The Vovinam fighting style ideally balances the use of "hard" energy (meeting an opponent's attack with force) and "soft" (using the enemy's own energy to deflect and destabilize him). As with other martial arts, the aim of Vovinam is to achieve effective results by employing minimal energy. The phrase "Iron hand over benevolent heart" is recited by Vovinam students.

Vovinam schools have been opened by disciples worldwide, but what better place to practice than here? Look up Clb Vovinam BTD in Hanoi, and a list of five Vovinam dojos in Saigon can be found at: www.atexpats.com/magazine/518-vietnamese-martial-arts.html

Water Puppets
Wait — this is cooler than it sounds. Water puppetry is a performance art that has been a pastime for over a millennium. Villagers in North Vietnam used to entertain the community by putting on puppet shows in flooded rice paddies.

Shows are performed today in a theatre, on a stage constructed above a waist-deep pool. A small orchestra with accompanying vocalists are positioned off to the side, while the puppeteers are hidden behind the backdrop. The puppets themselves are carved out of wood, then lacquered, painted and dressed up as characters from Vietnamese folklore. When it's time to perform, they're manipulated by bamboo rods and a network of underwater strings. Storylines are mined from daily village life, folklore legends and pages from the Vietnamese history books.

I saw a water puppet show at the Thang Long Theatre in Hanoi. I wasn't expecting much out what I assumed was just a rote, cliché tourist activity, but it was hard not to be impressed by the sheer complexity and showmanship that went into the performance. The stage lights strobe and flash, gongs are rung, and puppets dance in concert while dragons and giant fish zoom around them on the surface of the water.

And while I couldn't understand a damn thing, apparently the skits were heavy on the comedy, because the Vietnamese half of the audience couldn't stop laughing.

FESTIVALS AND PUBLIC HOLIDAYS

I'm still trying to get all Vietnam's celebrations in order, because the place has more than you can shake a bamboo stalk at. (If you count all the minor public holidays and regional or city-specific festivals, there are literally hundreds.)

What follows is a mostly complete list of the big ones, and I've expounded upon the more important ones later in the text. As you'll see, exact dates aren't always available, as long-standing Vietnamese holidays are based on the lunar calendar, and therefore tend to be mobile.

Calendar of Festivals and Public Holidays

Spring

- **International New Year's Day** (1 January)
  - The one you know and love: Resolutions and fireworks. Parties are held downtown—but I wouldn't go unless you're in the mood to stand in crowds for a few hours.
- **Founding of the Communist Party** (3 February)
- **Tet, or Lunar New Year** (Late January/Early February)
  - In Vietnam, this is the "real" New Year. See page 168 for more.
- **Hai Ba Trung Day** (6th day of the 2nd lunar month)
  - The anniversary of the Trung Sister's revolt against Chinese rule in AD 40. (Remember in the History chapter when I said to look this up? That exhortation still stands).
- **Holiday of the Dead** (Thanh Minh , 3rd day of 3rd lunar month)
  - A day to honor ancestors by visiting their tombs and sweeping them clean.
- **Death Anniversary of the Hung Kings** (Gio To Hung Vuong, 10th day of the 3rd lunar month)
  - A public holiday to memorialize the founding Kings of Vietnam. A huge celebration is held at Nghia Linh Mountain in Phu Tho province.
- **Reunification Day** (30 April)
  - The celebration of the fall of South Vietnam in 1975, which was the immediate catalyst for full Vietnamese Reunification of 1976.
- **International Labour Day** (1 May)
  - In keeping with its name, you still have to show up to work on this day.
- **Ho Chi Minh's Birthday** (19 May)

Summer

- **Day of Wandering Souls** (Trung Nguyen or Vu Lan, 14th /15th day of 7th lunar month)
  - Considered by some to be the second-most important festival in Vietnam. A day to go to the altars and offer food for the dead, lonely spirits who have no relatives to pray them.

Calendar of Festivals and Public Holidays

Autumn

- **Mid-Autumn Festival** (Tet Trung Phu, 15th day of the 8th lunar month)

  - Families celebrate the midpoint of the fall season (and the harvest moon). It's taken much more seriously in the countryside and smaller, outlying cities.

- **Independence Day** (2 September)

  - The anniversary of Uncle Ho's Declaration of Independence. School goes on recess, and a fair amount of the populace gets time off from work. Expect parades, fireworks, and congestion around major city landmarks—it's a great time for a day trip out to the country.

A dragon leaps between pillars during a Mid-Autumn Festival celebration.

- **Vietnamese Women's Day** (20 October)

  - Show the women in your life you appreciate them by giving them a floral bouquet.

- **Vietnamese Teacher's Day** (20 November)

  - Student and parents bring small gifts for their teachers at school. If their teachers have retired, students might visit them at their homes.

Winter

- **Confucius' Birthday** (Falls in either November or December)
- **Christmas** (25 December)

  - Yep, they have it here. Catholic cathedrals in the major cities hold midnight services, and the following day is observed by those of Judeo-Christian persuasion. The rest of the country carries on as they were, though; I have to report to work on Christmas Day for a 4pm class this year.

Tet

The alpha, king and grand-daddy of all Vietnamese holidays, Tet carries the celebratory action of Christmas and New Year's Day combined. It's a two-week festival that marks the arrival of spring, when the world comes alive again after the deadening effect of winter. Tet roves around a little, but will be sometime in late January or early February.

Vietnamese folk staying in the city will travel back to their hometowns so they can celebrate the festival with their families. They'll feast on *banh chung* (steamed rice cakes made with pork and green peas, and wrapped in green *la dong* leaves) and spring rolls, and drink rice wine.

Tet does double-duty as a family reunion, with the primary emphasis being on spending quality time with your kin. Gifts might be swapped (family members might give each other household or kitchen items), but my friends tell me that Tet hasn't yet been fully commercialized; you can't really describe it a Vietnamese Christmas.

But for those who have an income, Tet still costs something.

On The Scene for Tet

Tet changes everything, and makes every holiday I've ever experienced in my life so far seem like a casual joke. City-wide evacuations begin in the week leading up the holiday, with traffic jams plugging up the major roads at all hours. Families will pack themselves onto motorbikes, using ingenious lashing and balancing strategies in order to secure their baggage and the odd kumquat tree (to decorate the home with) onto their vehicles.

During the festival, nearly every business and institution in the country will shut for varying amounts of time. This year, my favourite café was closed for two days, while the school where I work took a full two weeks off.

If you're staying in 'Nam for Tet, stock up for it as if it were doomsday. Find out what day the festival officially begins and do a supply run in advance. (Not everything will be shuttered — you'll still have some restaurant options if you live near one of the tourist haunts.)

Adults (those out of school) slip lucky money, called *li xi*, into ornate red envelopes and hand it out to the kids in the family. Amounts vary, but it's said that the more lucky money you give a child, the more lucky breaks they can bank on over the next year. Older people get lucky money as well—the message behind this gift is that the hope they'll live longer.

Such reverent consideration of luck extends beyond currency; it's customary to not clean the home for the first three days (specifically, to not take out the trash). Wisdom holds that performing this chore might disrupt the household and the New Year's luck held within it. Also, almost every store in the country will be closed for business until the third day of Tet Festival.

Lastly, let's talk about gifts. If you're going to give one to a boss or colleague, do it before the first day of Tet. Everyone will have shipped off to their hometowns by the time the festival begins, and giving someone a gift when they come back to work will make it seem like you didn't bother thinking about them before the New Year.

What's an ideal gift? Just take a look around when you're outside—street vendors will be glad to help you out with this. You'll see big packages of tea, coffee, cookies, jam and whatever else stacked up on the sidewalk.

Day of Wandering Souls

Like the Holiday of the Dead (see page 166) this is another holiday of the supernatural consideration.

As the Vietnamese tell it, this is the day when the gates to the underworld are unchained and dead spirits, naked and hungry, fly back to their homes or villages to find a spread of food laid out on the family altar. Prayers are recited and paper money and clothing are burned. Why? That's how you transfer these items to the great beyond.

Now, those souls have somewhere to go — but many don't. Traditionally, the Vietnamese have prayed for the wandering, lonely souls who have no home to return to. It's said that without anywhere to go, they must instead float through the air on black clouds.

Beyond that, the Vietnamese memorialize those whose violent deaths made their bodies unrecoverable. One can imagine the amount of prayers that have been offered up for the millions of corpses stolen away by war. Sometimes the families who have been left behind will arrange empty graves called "windy tombs" (*ma gio*) so that the wandering spirit will have a place to rest.

The Vietnamese have long believed that amnesty and absolution of sins is possible in the afterlife, and The Day Of Wandering Souls is the best time for priests and relatives to pray and make their appeals on behalf of the dead.

And just as they are on Thanh Minh Festival, ancestor's altars and graves are cleaned on this day — a fact which just made me realize that a dead Vietnamese person's altar is cleaned far more often than my bedroom is. (Hey, I'm busy — you think writing a book is easy?)

Mid-Autumn Festival

A festival also celebrated in China, it's for families and villages to celebrate the harvest. As the full moon rises, children put on masks, carry lighted carp-shaped lanterns and tuck into some fruit and mooncakes. Drums are beaten, and dragon and lion dances are staged in the streets.

Besides being a time to thank the God of the Earth for the harvest bounty, Mid-Autumn is mostly for the kids — the emphasis is on them, because parents of past generations

Families take in a parade during Mid-Autumn Festival celebrations.

felt the need to make up for lost time with the little ones after being occupied with the harvest.

The cities of Hue and Hoi An hold lantern festivals, which are astonishing after dark — a coloured constellation of lanterns are strung over the streets and bridges.

In the cities, where the attitude is more business-like, you might not witness many celebrations there (I live in Hanoi, and the Mid-Autumn Festival passed by without me realizing). While I did drive by a single lion dance in the neighbourhood near my place, I didn't find out that it was related to the festival until weeks later. Maybe as the gears of development grind on, fewer and fewer Vietnamese feel connected to the traditions of a harvest festival.

RECREATION

In the cities, Vietnam does manage to balance out its cramped urban greyness with green spaces. You'll hear skateboard wheels clacking across the tiles, and badminton nets will be set up across the paths and sidewalks. Runners loop around the perimeters of the parks, while off the pathways, shirtless retirees perform push-ups and stretches. In the evenings, older women set up stereos, line up and engage in synchronized dances.

Look out for the Vietnamese hacky sack, especially in Saigon. Two or more people will face off, standing at what seems to be easily 20 metres apart, and they kick the hacky sack back and forth between them. Like tennis, the game's intent seems to be firing a shot your competition can't return. But here's why it's so impressive: Instead of kicking at the hacky as you would a soccer ball, they instead curl their foot behind their other leg, so that they meet the incoming projectile somewhere in their blind spot, and send it launching back at warp speed. Maybe the Vietnamese don't think much of this little game, but I find it to be a dazzling show.

Parks also function as informal language exchange hubs. You'll see foreigners on benches, working their way through this phrase or that in Vietnamese, with locals arrayed around

A man kicking a badminton shuttlecock in a Hanoi park.

them in Last Supper pose. I'd check out the following parks. Some are just green spaces, others have lakes, restaurants or small zoos.

If you're in Hanoi:

- **Cong Vien Nghia Do Park**(Cau Giay District),
- **Thong Nat Park** (Hai Ba Trung District),
- **Hanoi Zoological Garden Zoo & Park** (Ba Dinh District),
- **Hanoi Botanical Garden** (Ba Dinh District).

And Saigon:

- **Tao Dan Park** (District 1),
- **Le Van Tam Park** (District 1),
- **Hoa Binh Park** (District 5),
- **Van Thanh Park** (Bin Thanh District).

My recommendation is Turtle Lake, in Saigon's District 3. It's actually a pond, but there are curved pathways that take you over the water, as well as a few towers and platforms rising out of the centre of it. It's in the centre of a quiet roundabout a straight shot up the road from the Saigon Notre-Dame Basilica.

SPORTS

Football

Well, this isn't going to surprise you: Football, the globe's most captivating sport, is king here. Vietnamese devotees who can't even speak English can still list their favourite European players, and they'll wake up early to watch matches being played half a world away.

The French imported the game to Vietnam, and it's another spoil of victory that the Vietnamese have held onto

Vietnamese men playing a football game on a makeshift field in the countryside. (Photo credit: Kevin Abery)

throughout the post-colonial era. Most of the locals I talk to say that playing football is their go-to method for staying in shape. Make friends with them, and you might get a game invite at some point.

The Vietnamese Football Federation administers the country's teams and leagues. A number of foreign players have washed up ashore here in 'Nam and found spots on team rosters.

If you're in a city then you'll be able to find a live match. Don't expect a full stadium, but expect a lot of energy, face paint, singing and drum-banging.

Hanoi's team is the Ha Noi T&T Football Club and they play at the 22,500-seater Hang Day Stadium in Dong Da District. Saigon's team is the, uh, Ho Chi Minh City F.C., and their games are held at Thong Nhat Stadium in District 10. If you want to hit the pitch yourself, look up the expat football clubs Saigon Raiders, Saigon Hotshots, and Saigon Fusion.

Basketball

There is a pro hoop league here, but it'll be decades (if ever) before basketball catches up to football. It's gaining steam at the grassroots level, with high school and college students duking it out for pickup games on campus courts.

There's a whole mess of clubs and leagues to accommodate all the different skill levels. But if you want to play, it'll take a little digging, because you won't stumble upon it. Courts aren't as ubiquitous in public places as they are in the opposite hemisphere. (I've yet to see one in Hanoi, but in Saigon you'll of course have more luck). No matter where you are in the calendar, you probably won't be too far from an open tournament or dunk competition.

To get you started, the websites www.isport.com and www.courtsoftheworld.com both have online court finders. You'll have to pay a few thousand VND to get into some of them, and with others it's first-come-first-serve.

On the professional side of things, the sport seems to be barely out of its infancy. Vietnam's national team has had only middling success in regional competition and hasn't yet won a medal or an ASEAN championship. Meanwhile, the Vietnam Basketball Association was only founded in 2016, and as of this writing it's only comprised of five teams (right now the odds are pretty good for a championship, one should think).

Hanoi's team is the Buffaloes, with their southern nemesis being the Saigon Heat — which is also Vietnam's first professional basketball team. The Danang Dragons, Cantho Catfish, and Hochiminh (no, not a mistake — it's spelled as all one word) City Wings round out the bunch.

I personally think the team names are amazing (the Catfish!?), and am trying to carve out the time to go to a game, just to pick up a jersey.

Pro games in Hanoi are played at the Bach Khoa Arena, and in Saigon you can head over to the Canadian International School Arena in District 7. Tickets can be bought online via the team's English website.

But if we're speaking generally, the institution of Vietnamese professional sports has a few light-years to go before it achieves any sort of international legitimacy. Even in the big leagues, players take home a small paycheck. Making it into a foreign league is an absolute dream. Teachers and parents will join forces to dissuade their students' athletic ambitions.

Rugby

Most Vietnamese are unfamiliar with this sport, but expats have formed clubs in the major cities. They play other clubs based in Vietnam, and international matches are held as well. A five-second Facebook search should point you in the right direction, if you're looking to play. If you're just looking to watch some rugby, I can recommend Puku Bar & Café in Hanoi—it's open 24/7 and there's a big area up on the second floor with couches and flatscreens, where fans congregate in the early mornings to watch matches in Australia or South Africa or what have you. NFL games are screened, too. In Saigon, look up Hog's Breath Bar, Donkey Inn Saigon and D2 Sports Bar. (Google "sports pub" and you'll be off to the races.)

HOBBIES

Vietnamese people ask me what Americans do in their free time, and the correct answer is "everything". But some are more widespread and definitive than others, such as car restoration, hunting and marksmanship, fitness. Oh yeah,

Men play checkers on the street in Saigon.

one more thing—the worship of sport franchises, specifically football. What would the analogous pursuits in Vietnam be?

Well, they have the football fandom in common with us (we just disagree on what "football" actually is). But the similarities end there, at least for any Vietnamese who predate the millennial set. Consider the country's hectic history and the persistent poverty that has dogged its people for so long, and you might figure, correctly, that the country's array of hobbies is more limited.

As my Vietnamese friends tell it, older men like to collect ornamental plants and pet birds. Middle aged women, who've known a traditionalist upbringing, derive great pride from their cooking prowess. It's common small-talk ritual to detail the meals they've cooked for their families the previous evening. (If you want to impress the Vietnamese, learn to prepare some of their dishes.)

The younger generation draws on the benefits afforded them by an ever-opening society. Smartphone addiction is a clear and present danger (people will be scrolling their Facebook newsfeed while doing 40 km/h on a motorbike). And pet ownership is increasing, perhaps as furry surrogates for the children that modern twentysomethings haven't had yet. For those who aren't allowed to keep their own pets at home, there are cat and dog cafés in the major cities. Those exactly what they sound like: You sit there with your latte, and stroke the animals as they wander by.

Fitness culture is ascendant as well. And this isn't limited to the general cardio you get from pickup basketball — you'll see crossfit and muay thai studios here and there, too.

TRAVEL

At this point in the book, we've talked about the Big Cities of Hanoi and Saigon enough. Let's widen up our view a little bit.

Once you get going, travelling within 'Nam is a pretty easy, logical process. Remember that they want you (and your currency) to keep on flowing through the country. It doesn't matter where you're exploring. You can either take advantage of the structure offered by a tour, or just get a motorbike and a map, and choose your own adventure.

Note that this country has a hundred thousand little dead ends, national parks, jungle hamlets, and beach towns. You can never get to them all, but here's a top-to-bottom sprint you realistically can get to. Hit them all, and make sure you're never one-upped at a cocktail mixer by another traveller who's also done time in 'Nam. (Don't you hate it when that happens?)

Northern Vietnam
Sapa

Far up in the mountains, not so very far away from the Chinese border, is Sapa. You can probably get away with calling it Vietnam's Kathmandu; the active set uses it as a staging area to strike out and hike Fansipan, the tallest mountain in the country (and taller than any peaks in Cambodia and Laos,

The open roads outside the city.

also). If you're not a hiker, then you can just rent a motorbike and fishtail down the dirt road into the villages where some of the hill tribes live. You can't miss them; they still wear the traditional dress. If you're not a biker, just stay up in the town of Sapa proper; sit among the clouds, and have a few dozen rounds of coffee while you stare at the peaks. The view has an astonishing, narcotic quality to it.

Sapa is on every tourist's hit list, and deserves its spot there. It's a six-hour bus ride from Hanoi, and about nine hours by train.

Halong Bay

A UNESCO World Heritage site, this is probably the number-one tour stop that everyone does. You take a cruise through

Homestays

If you're a country mouse and the urban crush doesn't quite do it for you, then what you can do is take a deep dive into traditional Vietnamese culture with a homestay.

Vietnam has an eco-tourism winner with these. What you can do is arrange to stay with a village family, who'll put you up in a hut, cook and serve your meals, and during the day you can either sit quietly in the hut, or take a trek around the vicinity. Sapa (a mountain town a six-hour drive north from Hanoi) is famous for these. When you book a tour up there, you'll also be offered the homestay option.

I actually haven't done one in Sapa (because I'm a contrarian). However, some friends and I did do a homestay in a little area called Lang Xat, which sits about 100 miles southwest of Hanoi. We motorbiked there on the Ho Chi Minh Highway, and stayed for two nights in a village clustered around a waterfall. We had a guide was with us for the whole trip, who took use hiking up the giant steps of the rice terraces.

It was a completely frills-free experience: Sleeping in a hut raised up on stilts, relieving ourselves in an old-school outhouse, taking ice-cold showers (the "shower heads" were actually just toilet bidet spray guns, mounted higher up on the wall than usual), and sitting in the woods with a book, enjoying the quietude and the fact that we had exactly nowhere to be. I liked pulling in deep breaths of clean mountain air, imagining that my lungs were regenerating from the atmospheric trauma they routinely suffer in the city. For two nights in the jungle, we paid a little over one million VND each. The village verged on completely inaccessible — it might as well have been on the mountains of Mars. Arrival required motorbiking up a steep track of rocks that stuck out of the dirt like saw blades (our convoy stopped three times to fix flats.)

Only a small slice of tourists go through such an inconvenient trek, but the locals seemed fine with the pace of business. Over dinner, as our host family plied us with rice wine, we drew out our phones and had a choppy conversation with our guide over Google Translate. She told us that a few officials from the National Tourist Administration had just been up to the village — they know it's a hot draw, and they're trying to figure out ways to truck in even more tourists from the urbanities. This would require the imposition of new roads, which would bring in van after van of city-slickers, who would want modern upgrades for their stay.

But our guide said, "We don't need new technology. We have a waterfall."

and around hundreds of islands and karsts dotted throughout the bay. The view is astonishing no matter the weather or time of day, but at the golden hour of sunset the scenery is lit and coloured in such a way that you might lose your mind. From Hanoi it's a three-hour drive east.

The bay's also known for the legendary tourist haven of Cat Ba Island. That's where you can park yourself for a night or two of simulated retirement by way of the beach-chair lifestyle.

The "cruise ships" on the bay actually match your mental image of a Chinese junk. There are day cruises, but for longer ones, you can book a cabin on board.

Words of warning: There are, oh, about a million Halong Bay tours, but try to vet yours beforehand. The boats might not arrive and depart on schedule, and your on-deck cabin that's advertised as having AC might not actually have AC. And as I said, everyone hits up Halong Bay — and that includes hordes of backpackers, many of them recent college graduates or gap-year ragers, who haven't yet dialed back on the partying. Your boat could likely devolve into a floating frat house, and should you be held hostage in such a scenario, then you have my sympathies.

Ninh Binh

This place is lesser-known, and so doesn't get quite as much love as the two aforementioned destinations. But Ninh Binh still deserves its own share of ink in this book. It's a city (and province) on the coast, about two hours south of Hanoi. If you have a day and need to get away from the capital, look this place up.

In Ninh Binh, there's the Bai Dinh temple complex, which houses the largest Buddha in Southeast Asia, as well as a few pagodas laid atop misty mountain ridges. For a look at the Judeo-Christian side of things, look up the Phat Diem Cathedral, a church that was erected in the Oriental style back in the 19th century.

If you're like me and take the "seen one, seen 'em all" approach to houses of worship, then take the river tour that's right outside the city. You load up in a wooden boat, and local women row you (they push the oars with their feet) through a series of caves and down a waterway with cliffs and deep-green hills rising up around you.

If you're there on a pre-paid tour, the rower's fee will be included. But since they work hard to push you (and a few dozen other tourists that day) up the river and back, leaving them a tip is encouraged.

Ba Vi National Park

A respite from the city can be found here, in a huge park that's about a 40km drive west of Hanoi. Trekking routes take you through cloudy forests, teeming with wildlife. There're also the ruins of an abandoned resort project undertaken long ago by the French. Thick tree cover lends the park an ethereal quality and keeps a hush in the air.

A trio of 1,200m peaks from the Ba Vi Mountain Range have been captured within Ba Vi's borders. Stone steps are laid into the earth of the trails, and on the hike up you'll go past the pagodas and temples sitting quietly along the slopes. Get out of Hanoi early enough, and you can summit one of the peaks and be back in the city in time for dinner.

Beyond all that, Ba Vi's territory includes a few campsites, a water park, and clear-water lakes for fishing.

Central Vietnam
Danang

Somewhere around the approximate midpoint of this long country sits Danang. It's Vietnam's third largest city, but don't get too excited. If we're talking size and population, it's a steep dropoff from Hanoi and Saigon. There's just one building you might consider a skyscraper.

It was once a French port city, and during the war it was partitioned within South Vietnam. US forces used it then as a hinge from which to strike up and down the coast and into the country. Danang is still urban Vietnam, but with only a shade over one million inhabitants, it doesn't have the oppressive bustle you suffer through in the "Terrible Twins" of Hanoi and Saigon. Danang's metronome sweeps at a slower tempo, and its volume is turned down a few precious notches.

Danang can come off as pretty bland, but is saved by the beauty on its fringes. It is at once a beach, river, and mountain

Dragons watch over Danang's Han River.

Tourists working their way though Hoi An's Old Town.

town. In the summer, the resorts are packed. During the off-season, when it gets cold and the weather gets dreary, take a walk out among the fishing boats moored on sand and watch the outlines of cargo ships lumbering along out there in mist. There are a few cool bridges over the Han River. One of them looks like a dragon; another is a grand suspension bridge.

If you're in the market for Instagram likes, then listen up. A little way outside the city proper there's a resort called Ba Na Hills, and they offer a 5km cable car that sends you up into the peaks. And driving 15 minutes south of the city centre brings you to the Marble Mountains, which aren't actually mountains but rather a quintet of limestone towers named after the five ancient elements. A 10-minute hike puts you up on a tiny summit about the size of a helipad. Standing there, you'll behold the ocean, downtown Danang, and a pagoda in the dip between two of the mountains. This is the Mount Olympus, God's eye vantage point that will fulfil your shutterbug urges for a little while.

The stone steps of the Marble Mountain trail aren't an obvious find from the road, but if you keep your eyes open you'll see a tall glass tube that's out of place with its natural surroundings—that's an elevator that lets you skip the short hike.

Keep travelling, because there's more to see. Danang acts as a transitional hub if you're on your way out to the smaller cities of Hoi An and Hue.

Hoi An

Your primary motivation for heading here will probably be to see the Old Town, a preserved zone of space that's a UNESCO World Heritage site (along with Halong Bay and five others in Vietnam).

Homes constructed during the Chinese and French dominions still stand on the canals. A covered bridge (a Japanese installation) is placed over the water and at dark, red lanterns glow above the roofs. You'll see the vendors and realize that the place has been commercialized—payment of a small fee is required to gain access to Old Town in the first place—but you'll be able to trick yourself into thinking you're walking around in the past. It's an absolute contrast to the featureless streets of Danang.

Hoi An has no airport of its own, but it's only 30km south of Danang.

My Son

Moving inward off the coast, you'll hit the jungle and soon reach My Son. It's not a city, it's holy ground—a cluster of Hindu temples built by the Champa people. The Champa (a collective term applied to the myriad number of smaller Cham groups) were a regional power here until the newly-insurgent Vietnamese state annexed them in the 19th century.

Champa ideology and architecture were informed by Indian and Cambodian cultures, which is why their constructs don't remind you of anything else in Vietnam. The temples, now faded, chipped and mossy, were devoted to the worship of the god Shiva. Built between the 4th and 14th centuries, they're fossils of a forgone empire. Accordingly, My Son has been declared a UNESCO site.

There are 18 structures standing today, but there used to be 70; the rest of the complex was destroyed by American bombers during the war. The blast craters are still visible, and limited, careful restoration efforts are ongoing.

Note that most tours of the complex start from Danang or Hoi An.

Hue

Further bolstering Central Vietnam's vacationing cred is the city of Hue. The city was the country's capital and the seat of the Imperial Court from 1802 until 1945.

On the strength of its giant pagoda and royal tombs, Hue has joined the UNESCO club as well. There's also the Imperial Citadel, a place so closely derived from China's Forbidden City that China should have sued for copyright infringement. Like My Son, Hue took on some heavy damage during the war, so what you're looking at is a shattered facsimile of the place's historic grandeur. But even in this state, it remains astounding.

The weather is hit and miss (with the rain hitting more often than it misses) but when it holds off, take a bicycle and weave through the city on it, and head up the Perfume River, too.

If you're a war historian intending on making a pilgrimage out to the site of the Khe Sanh Combat Base (the site of the war's biggest single battle), then you can arrange to head there from Hue.

Unlike Hoi An, you can reach Hue by both air and rail.

The South
Nha Trang

Head south of Danang and work down the coast toward Saigon, and you'll encounter Nha Trang.

I canvassed a few dozen Vietnamese people and asked them where their favourite spot in the country was. Nha Trang was a common denominator. It's a beach city (emphatically stated to be Vietnam's best) of about 400,000, where resorts have spawned to serve the waves of foreign and local tourists who wash up on the white sands down there.

In case long days of languid tanning aren't your thing,

there are some extracurricular options presented by the rice terraces nearby and the mountains hovering above the city. You can also go scuba diving and get down a little bit at some of the dance clubs that stay open past the dreaded Vietnamese curfew of zero dark thirty.

The city also has a theme park on an island off the coast called Vinpearl Land, if you feel like trying out a Vietnamese approximation of Disneyland. There's a cable car ride operated by the park that pulls you out to the island.

You can fly into Cam Ranh Airport, 30km removed from downtown Nha Trang. Just avoid the city from October to January, when the rain is pouring.

For more island adventures in the South, look up Phu Quoc Island. And more beach cities include Mui Ne and Vung Tau.

Dalat

Going inland a bit, we come to the Central Highlands and the city of Dalat.

This is a city the French colonists once fashioned as a resort. Their villas are, you guessed it, still there. (The Vietnamese kicked out the French, but rather like the buildings that they left behind.) It's as if the French, missing their own Alps, tried to recreate the environment here in Southeast Asia. And it would have worked, too—if it ever snowed here.

Since you can't go skiing in Dalat, go for a waterfall hike or a rumble on a mountain bike instead. The views up here are transcendental; you won't miss the powder.

There are bright street markets within Dalat itself, and pine forests rest outside the town. The area has the quiet, textured vistas to draw in honeymooners, and the tranquillity to help you along on your spiritual journey, if that's the kind of thing you're after. There's also a cable car (this country is full of them, doesn't it seem?) that brings you up to the Thien Vien Truc Lam Monastery. Beyond that, there's the serenity of Xuan Hong Lake, right in the middle of town. Oh, and with its coffee plantations, Dalat is also probably where your morning joe comes from.

You get into the city via bus, train or plane.

Mekong Delta

We're almost to the end. Go straight west out of Saigon, and you'll verge into the Mekong Delta.

This is actually an entire region, where the landmass called Vietnam first lifts itself out of the sea, and in turn where the Mekong River splits into tributaries which then siphon themselves into the Gulf of Thailand and the South China Sea. The geography is crazy: islands, hills, glades, forests, plains, twisty waterways, and villages built on silt

A merchant rows up a river of the Mekong Delta. (Photo credit: Kevin Abery)

and sediment. Tours can help you make sense of it all, and guide you through a cross-section of it.

Being such a vast, inter-provincial spread, there's a plethora of avenues from which to attack the Delta. But for simplicity's sake, most people choose the city of Can Tho as their base of operations. The city has its own international airport, if you want to bypass Saigon.

You could lose an afternoon with the floating market, called Cai Rang, which on the edge of the city. Scores of wooden boats, piloted by entrepreneurs in rice hats, and loaded up with flowers and textiles and every kind of fruit you've ever seen, heave and sway on the water.

CHAPTER 8

LANGUAGES

> **❛**We should learn languages,
> because language is the only thing
> worth knowing even poorly.**❜**

— **Kato Lomb, translator and interpreter**

COMMUNICATING IN ENGLISH

Locals are used to monolingual foreigners. Tourists stride through, speaking English to anyone they come across—nationality matters not—just as toddlers direct their gibberish every which way.

Many Vietnamese working in the service industry have adapted and can talk shop, name prices and haggle in English. And while common English fluency is a long way off (there's a reason you can achieve gainful employment within the ESL industry here), many Vietnamese urbanites know enough phrases that you'll never necessarily need to learn the language. Many choose not to, and to each their own.

Now, what I find annoying are the Westerners who shout at the locals in English, as if the Vietnamese are unintelligent by virtue of not being native English speakers, or as if it's possible to elicit understanding of a foreign tongue through sheer volume. It annoys the Vietnamese, too. As an immigrant here, I can say shouting won't do you any favours.

What will earn you some favours is learning at least the pleasantries in Vietnamese. Go beyond the basic phrase book, and you may start provoking mild astonishment.

Once, in a café, I ordered tea by using the Vietnamese word (*tra*), and the staff behind the register actually clapped. I'm at least halfway sure they weren't being sarcastic. I prefer to think that they appreciated the effort, since foreigners, on the whole, make little.

While we're on the subject of appreciation, I've received this curious compliment a few times from my students: "Wow, your English is very good!"

COMMUNICATING IN VIETNAMESE

Some expats arrive and make a real effort at assimilation, thereby provoking insecurity in the rest of us. There's a South African expat I've met who's been in Hanoi for less time than I have, and every now and then I spot him in the market having a fast-paced conversation in Vietnamese with a local guy over bowls of *pho*.

How did he learn? By sitting down and talking with the locals. For the sake of my ego, I privately hoped that he was a linguist, and mastering multiple languages was his forte.

"I'm not a polyglot, I just try to adapt to where I'm at," he told me. "Speak English, you're speaking to their heads. Speak Vietnamese, and you're speaking to their hearts."

I'm still struggling to get to his level. After nine months of practice, my pronunciation still comes off as if I suffer from a speech impediment. The only thing that's understood consistently is *bia*, because it's easy to say, commonly used, and sounds like how they say "beer" in Boston. All of this is to say that my hat's off to you if you've made substantial inroads with the Vietnamese language, and they understand what you're saying.

LEARNING VIETNAMESE (PREPARE FOR INFERIORITY)

Studying Vietnamese feels like trying to make sense of calculus when you haven't learned how to count yet. I've found it requires a significant commitment of brainpower to make any sort of headway. My own progress with the language has moved at a glacial pace. (My excuse is that I'm an American, and Americans generally do not take up the practice of language learning.) But things are moving. By the time this book is published, I should have achieved the linguistic proficiency of a three-year-old.

Anyway, here are some notes on communicating in Vietnam, cobbled together after spending the better part of a year repeatedly smashing into the Vietnamese language barrier at top speed.

The Written Language

Modern Vietnamese is written using most of the letters from the Roman alphabet.

I say "most of" because they don't use f, j, w, or z.

Vietnamese used to be transcribed using Mandarin Chinese hanzi characters (remember China's casual 1,000-year pit stop in 'Nam), but the drawback was that a Vietnamese person first needed to learn Mandarin, in order to be able to understand the characters, before they could finally gain access to their own language — a process which was exactly as annoying as it sounds.

This multi-levelled restriction on literacy held fast until Jesuit missionaries sailed into a Vietnamese port in the 17th century. Keen on getting as many people literate as possible (for evangelical purposes), they developed the Portuguese-based *quoc ngu* writing system, and that's why you'll see Roman letters written all over Vietnam today. (When the French took over, they imposed the *quoc ngu* throughout the whole nation).

Great! you think. Familiar lettering. This odyssey isn't going to be that bad.

The Vietnamese Alphabet

Vietnamese doesn't use all of the Roman letters, but they still have more letters than we do. For example, they have what appears to be three different "A"s. The alphabet has 29 letters and 12 of them are vowels.

Here they are, along with IPA (International Phonetic Alphabet) symbols, which is my gift to all you linguists out there.

- Aa (/aːˈɕ/)
- Ăă (/aːˈꜛꜙ/)
- Ââ (/əːˈꜛꜙ/)
- Bb (/ɓeˈɕ, ɓəːˈꜛꜙ/)
- Cc (/seˈɕ, kəːˈꜛꜙ/)
- Dd (/zeˈɕ, zəːˈꜛꜙ/)
- Đđ (/ɗeˈɕ, ɗəːˈꜛꜙ/)
- Ee (/ɛˈɕ/)
- Êê (/eˈɕ/)
- Gg (/zeˈɕ, ɣəːˈꜛꜙ/)
- Hh (/hatˈꜙ, həːˈꜛꜙ/)
- Ii (/iˈꜙ, iˈɕ ŋanˈꜙꜙ/)
- Kk (/kaˈɕ/)
- Ll (/(ɛ ɭ)ləːˈꜛꜙ/)
- Mm (/(ɛmˈɕ)məːˈꜛꜙ/)

- Nn (/(ɛnˈɕ)nəːˈꜛꜙ/)
- Oo (/ɔˈɕ/)
- Ôô (/oˈɕ/)
- Ơơ (/əːˈɕ/)
- Pp (/peˈɕ, pəːˈꜛꜙ/)
- Qq (/kuˈɕ, kwiˈɕ, kwəːˈꜛꜙ/)
- Rr (/ɛˈɭɹəːˈꜛꜙ, zəːˈꜛꜙ/)
- Ss (/ɛtˈꜙꜙsiˈɕꜙ, ʂəːˈꜛꜙ/)
- Tt (/teˈɕ, təːˈꜛꜙ/)
- Uu (/uˈɕ/)
- Ưư (/ɨˈɕ/)
- Vv (/veˈɕ, vəːˈɕ/)
- Xx (/ikˈꜙꜙsˈɕꜙꜙ, səːˈꜛꜙ/)
- Yy (/iˈɕza:jˈɕꜙ, iˈɕkəːˈꜛꜙɛtˈꜙꜙ/)

Well, you're going to find out pretty fast that the Roman lettering is but a deceptive lure. The letters won't help you much, because sounding out Vietnamese words phonetically tends to be a nonstarter. The reason for this? Vietnamese syllables have been crunched into a lettering system that wasn't designed to accommodate them, which means that letters produce a different sound than you could have ever thought possible. For example, a "d" can be pronounced like a "z" in the North. But in the South, it's pronounced as a "y".

So, at first pass, the language remains just as impenetrable and alien as any other. Some of the syllables are a queer bunch (well, they seem that way to us) because they must be produced far back in the throat or up in the high reaches of the nasal cavity in order to be pronounced properly.

There are also little marks and squiggles hovering above certain letters and certain times. Those are diacritical marks. They change the tone of the word. You've probably heard of tones—how pronouncing a word with a different stress or lilt can change its entire meaning. The world's most widely-spoken tonal language is Mandarin, with four tones.

Vietnamese? It has six.

So, depending on how you say the word *ma*, for example, it can mean six different things: Ghost, mother, which, tomb, horse, or rice seedling.

Tones

Now it's time to familiarize yourself with the six tones that will, in short order, become the bane of your existence. The tone's definition and pronunciation instructions have been included as well.

- a (flat, high-level): The only tone with no tone marker—imagine your voice as a flat, horizontal line on a graph.
- à (flat, low-level): It says "flat," but the tone actually descends just a little bit. Not a sharp drop, though.
- ã (non-flat, high falling-rising tone): Huh? Here it is in English: The syllable should make short drop, then a very short pause, followed by a quick rise. Do it all from a higher register. Easiest thing ever, right?
- ả (non-flat, low falling-rising): With this one, the tone should fall quickly, and then rise. Do it from a lower register.
- á (non-flat, high rising): The tone marker gives you the right idea. The syllable should make a quick, sharp rise, just like you lift the last word of an English sentence when you ask a question.
- ạ (non-flat, low falling): A sharp drop, but performed at a lower register—think of a kid trying to imitate the voice of a gruff man.

Just do yourself a favour, and don't simply try these at home—jump on YouTube to see if you're saying them right. There are a few dozen videos devoted to demystifying Vietnamese tones.

Vietnamese regional dialects differ as dialects do all over the world. But apparently they only use five tones in the South (they have a hybrid pronunciation of ã and ả). Some Northerners accuse Southerners of doing this out of laziness. (Because having only five tones is incredibly lazy.)

COMMUNICATING WITH THE VIETNAMESE
Non-verbal Communication

So, you're progressing with the difficult mastery of pronunciation and tones. But wait, there's more!

Sure, words matter. But non-verbal cues form the scaffolding of most human communication. Here are some notes on using them in Vietnam.

- You've probably heard that eye contact is an indicator of strength and confidence. And that's exactly why you shouldn't use it over here—at least when you're talking to one of your elders, or someone of higher status than you. They might view it as a challenge or an affront to their status. (I mean, you can look at someone older than you, but be mindful of laser-focusing your gaze into theirs).

- There's also silence to consider. In a conversation, Vietnamese don't really give you verbal prods like "yeah" and "uh-uh" while you're speaking. They'll simply sit there, receptive, mouths closed and ears open. They might give a few nods, but not much more. If their arms are crossed while listening, that's good. We see that gesture as one of boredom or insecurity, but here it's more respectful. When I first starting teaching Vietnamese adults, my classes were hushed and quiet as a crypt. My students rarely reacted or looked right at me. To me, it felt like I was bombing in front of a tough crowd, but they were actually just listening.

- You can kick back and relax in public, but it's rude to point the bottom of your foot at someone, so keep the soles on the floor until you get home. (With your family or dear friends, it's OK). But with everyone else, showing them the bottom of your foot is the apparent equivalent of walking past someone in the West with your middle finger up.

- Never touch someone — especially an adult — on the head. With children, this isn't welcomed but it's somewhat acceptable.

- And as chummy as you might feel with them, don't pat someone of higher status on the back.

- Avoid putting your hands in your pockets while talking. This can seem arrogant.

- Don't feel slighted if a Vietnamese person simply smiles in response when you compliment them — a knee-jerk thank you isn't part of their social programming. That's not the only pleasantry they skip over. Smiles can be substituted for "hello" and "I'm sorry" too, which can create even more silences that'll feel awkward and almost cult-like until you get used to them.

- If you want to beckon someone over to you, don't wave or make a "come on over" motion. What you should do instead is put out your hand, palm down, and move your fingers up and down a few times. And only do this to someone your age or younger; people won't come over if they're of higher status than you.

- And while we're on the subject of hand-flapping, let's talk about traffic. You know how to signal a turn while you're driving, right? Well, not here, you don't — technology has nothing to do with it. Usually the passenger on the back of the motorbike will stick an arm out straight and waggle their hand up and down, as if experiencing a localized seizure or playing an invisible piano. It looks pretty dumb, but it gets

your attention—and it's the only thing that works. Traffic is too frantic and chaotic for a weak bike blinker to get any notice.

All right—I know that was a lot of information. But note that flubbing some of these gestures won't land you in hot water with the younger generation. They have more empathy toward outsiders. It's the elders who still live by tradition. While we're talking about the old-timers: Go with a short bow when you meet them. It shows respect.

Addressing Others

We've got a few more complications here. Depending on your relationship to your conversation partner, you have to use different markers to address them. The Vietnamese will cut you some slack, but remember that status is important, and some folks will be irked if a foreigner refers to them as a child.

It'll take some practice for you to figure out where to plug these identifiers in, but here's a cheat sheet:

- **Em** is a word for someone younger than you are—and generally a female. (I once thanked a middle-aged shopkeeper by saying "Cảm ơn em", and his daughter shouted at me for referring to him as a little girl.)

- **Con** is a word for a child. Let's practice—how do you say thanks to a child? Did you say "Cảm ơn con?" Well done.

- **Bạn:** Friend.

- **Anh:** Older brother, or a male who's older than you are. (It almost sounds like "ang".)

- **Chị:** Older sister or older female.

- **Bác:** Reserved for someone older than you are (male or female), usually of middle-age. The rough equivalent of "sir" or "madam".

- **Chú:** A man older than you but whom you feel deserves a more reverent word than the catch-all **anh**.

- **Cô:** A woman at least a decade older than you—but who's still younger than a...

- **Bà:** A grandmother or elderly madam.

- **Ông:** Elderly gentleman.

That's a lot of information—it feels like memorizing a bunch of code names. But as a foreigner, you can get away with calling anyone **ban** (friend), and you'll be fine.

To summon someone, or get their attention, you use the right identifier, followed by the word **ơi**. (Pronounce it as you would the "oy" in "oy vey".) For example, if I'm calling out to a man who's older than I am, I'll say **anh ơi**. Friends are **ban ơi**, and so on and so forth.

CHAPTER 9

WORKING IN THE COUNTRY

*❝I like work; it fascinates me.
I can sit there and look at it for hours.❞*

— Jerome K. Jerome, writer

If your tour of duty over here is long enough—and if you want to keep eating—then sooner or later you'll enter the Vietnamese business world. Wherever you work, be it at a Vietnamese or Western company, the staff will probably consist of mixed company, so the odds are low that you'll be the lone foreigner in the office.

THE IMMIGRANT WORKFORCE

Many expats in their 30s or older hold financial or government posts. The Vietnamese are aware that these foreign professionals who move over here likely bring home more than enough bacon, and that they have the skills to justify their international deployment.

Then there are the backpackers, the hordes of twentysomethings who touch down at the international airports each day. Many of them, being native English speakers, use the country as a pit stop to reload the travel coffers. These drifter teachers (of which I am one) can be embraced as employable resources, and treated well in exchange for their efforts. That, or they can be viewed as interchangeable opportunists and therefore taken advantage of. It's all about who you work for (and how good your work ethic is).

The Vietnamese know that if you're a wanderer, money

can be tight—they're also aware that the ridiculously high standard of living you enjoy here is something you probably won't be able to replicate back in your home country.

"We actually assume that a lot of foreigners don't have too much money," another Vietnamese friend said. "That's why they're here, in a cheap country."

But—regardless of how much money you have—a lot of locals still wouldn't mind trading places with you. Your relative means and Western passport are superpowers that clear away border fences. Some students of mine, who've never once been abroad (and need to secure reputable employment if they're to do so) once gave me a weird look when I tactlessly mentioned that I've "only" been to 10 countries in my travels.

WORKING HOURS

Your average Vietnamese workday lasts eight hours, from about eight in the morning to six in the evening.

Now wait a minute, Ben. Isn't that 10 hours?

It is—but you have to remember the two-hour lunch break. It lasts from about 12pm to 2pm. In Vietnam, lunch is a long, quiet, sacred oasis of downtime, perfect for a siesta. If you stop by a street restaurant or shop after 1pm, they might be closed because the workers are all napping.

Government workers start the day quicker but also burn out faster. The doors will usually open at about 7.30am, and everyone goes home at 4.30pm. Keep this in mind for when you have official business to get done.

Following the school schedule, many Vietnamese businesses run six days a week, with workers reporting to the office from Monday to Saturday—leaving just one precious day a week for rest and recovery.

ATTIRE

There are no real surprises here; most professional Vietnamese take pride in their workplace appearance. Business casual is good for day-to-day office wear. If there's a meeting, a jacket can't hurt.

I visited the office of a Vietnamese IT company and the workers' dress code was relaxed. A few people were in jeans and collared shirts. The one inviolable golden rule seems to be: no T-shirts.

If you're an English teacher, you can get away with a polo shirt and jeans.

IT'S ALL ABOUT WHO YOU KNOW

If you're of the white-collar persuasion, keep a few of your evenings open. Business relationships here are predicated far more on personal and social connections than you might be used to in the West, where you can't go wrong with a semi-detached, all-business workplace persona.

In Vietnam there are fewer barriers between your social and professional lives. A friend of mine who manages a Hanoi-based company said there's almost never a contract signing unless you've at least had dinner or drinks with the other party first. An office meeting or quick business lunch doesn't cut it; people like to connect with each other outside of the pressurized atmosphere of the workplace.

The Wooing Process

It's an unstated given that whoever shows the client the best time will essentially be a lock to earn the contract. Prospect clients expect a nice night out, with a few venue changes. This means that after the restaurant, you'll take them to more bars than there are on a monkey gym, with perhaps a stopover at

The Workplace

Common courtesy will go a long way with your colleagues, but it also can't hurt to do a little homework so you can short-circuit the awkward cultural collisions before they happen.

Dos

- Make a real effort to be punctual. Everyone empathizes with a bad traffic story, but it's also expected you'll build extra time into your commute to counteract the gridlock, especially for important engagements. Traffic here is never a surprise.

- Help the rest of us foreigners look good by at least learning how to exchange pleasantries in Vietnamese.

- When you get better at speaking Vietnamese, remember that you address superiors by their title or designation (manager, director, etc.), followed by their family name. Status is earned and revered here; you'll do well to show respect for it.

- Double and triple check on an arrangement to see that it's going through as planned. People get busy and agreements go forgotten (sometimes accidentally, sometimes not).

Don'ts

- Balk at personal questions. The Vietnamese will ask "How old are you?", "Do you have a girlfriend? Why not?", "Have you gained weight?" or "How much money do you make?" Those questions are their way of taking an interest in and fast-tracking their familiarity with you—being forthright isn't rude.

- Overuse sarcasm. Western humour can be drier than a Saltine, and the Vietnamese may not realize you're joking.

- Be surprised at passive aggression (or curiously inefficient communication) For example: Rather than raise their hands and tell me what they're thinking, most students of mine would rather write down feedback, submit it to an admin in the school office, and wait for it to work its way down the chain of command to me. Similarly, there have been a few times when I've said good-bye to my boss, walked out of the building, and felt my phone shudder as I receive an "urgent" email from the same boss I'd just been talking to.

- Disrespect Ho Chi Minh. Vietnam is like anywhere else; people like to complain about the government. You can join in and share your observations, but know that mentioning the big man himself might touch a nerve.

a karaoke joint if everyone's feeling jovial enough. Go out with business contacts, and you might be out until the witching hour. (Too bad you need to be back at work by 9am.)

But it's Not All Business…

…the Vietnamese like to hang out, too.

You'll get semi-regular dinner or coffee invites from colleagues. Up in Hanoi, I've been the token foreigner at a fair amount of meet-ups, and I almost always have a great time (except when I sense I've only been invited for free English tutoring. Gutting through a meal's worth of elementary small talk is a draining experience).

Once you're all sitting down, you have to read the room and figure out how to proceed as the odd one out. I chat to whoever's next to me, taking the conversation to its fullest cordial extent. The Vietnamese are unfailingly polite, and they're interested in you—but I've also sensed that it's important not to monopolize all of their attention. They've invited you out because they don't want to exclude you, but keep in mind that they're speaking to you in their second language. That can make them feel like they're on the spot, so I try to pull back periodically to let them downshift and turn to their Vietnamese friends.

Anyway, while the rest of the table is carrying on in Vietnamese, your job will be to smile and wait it out. I usually try to appear as if the task of using chopsticks requires my utmost concentration.

When you're drinking, this is how you say cheers: "*mot, hai, ba* (one, two, three) yo!" The more booze in your system, the louder you yell it.

Pro-tip: There's always a one-off party trick you can use that'll amp up the evening a bit. Point to objects in the room and ask your coworkers, "How do you say this in Vietnamese? And what about this?" The more they're drinking, the more excited they'll get. Grown men will slap the table and keel over laughing as you flub the tones and pronunciation. I say that you can only use this trick once, because they'll expect you to remember the Vietnamese words they give you.

MANAGING VIETNAMESE WORKERS

Working in a new culture can make you feel like you're cutting against the grain of it—and some expats who oversee Vietnamese staff report that they've had to be very hands-on at work.

"A lot of my job is micro-managing," my friend—the one who manages a company in Hanoi—says. "My staff follows instructions exactly to the letter. You'll get no less, but also not anything more, than what you ask of them."

He once asked a worker to bring him a price estimate for a computer server, which the worker did. Later, doing some research, my friend found a better server price on offer from a different company. He asked his worker if he'd seen that there was a lower price listed online.

"Yes," said the worker.

"Why didn't you show it to me?" my friend asked.

"Oh, I'm very sorry. You only asked me to bring you one estimate," the worker said. It never crossed the guy's mind to locate the best price—he was only thinking about showing his boss one price, any price. And in his mind, that was a job well done.

"But once we're all on the same page, my staff gets their work done on time," my friend told me. "Vietnamese people don't like working overtime."

This is one example of where Vietnam differs from the long

working hours that are rampant in Japan or South Korea.

Another manager said that he's begun writing extremely vague job descriptions when hiring. He was running into problems with workers who wouldn't perform tasks that hadn't been explicitly listed in the description, sometimes leaving him with no one to work on a certain project. He had to add a bullet point that said something to the effect of "assist the management with any and all tasks necessary for project completion".

Teamwork is, apparently, a radical new idea for some workers. In some offices there's a mentality of "Why should I help him? That's his job." The idea of everyone working together (to keep the company in the black, so that everyone keeps getting paid) might actually need to be spelled out.

Worker turnover can be quite high, and bosses who want to counteract this have to be deliberate about building an office culture. They might prop up worker rapport by organizing a company soccer team or going out for drinks at least once a month.

Starting a Business

Here are a couple of links for those of you with an entrepreneurial bent:

- Information from the World Bank: www.doingbusiness.org/data/exploreeconomies/vietnam/starting-a-business
- And from Global Business Services: www.gbs.com.vn/index.php/en/faq/business-registration/171-guide

---

IMAGE

Let's flip back to prejudice for a second. There are a few Facebook groups for expats that function as informal online job fairs. (The groups du jour change frequently, but when I was a fresh fish, "Hanoi Massive" was all the rage.) It's on these pages that foreigners trying to chase down a job will post a message outlining their qualifications, and local employers will similarly post when they're looking for workers.

It's semi-routine to see a school advertise for "American or European-looking" native English teachers. Read between the lines and prepare to be outraged, because the "American or European" qualifier is a Trojan horse for what they really want, which is "white skin".

Now before you sharpen your pitchforks and come running, I've seen this in China and Korea, too. Such blatant screening is acceptable in this hemisphere. Some ads actually specify "white teachers only".

And while it's unfair, there's no recourse for those who get passed over on basis of race or appearance. There aren't really any anti-discrimination laws akin to those pasted on office walls in the West.

Nice Work, If You Can Get It

In what's probably a bid to present a multinational image, Vietnamese companies will hire white foreigners to sit in on business meetings with them. What do you have to do? Absolutely nothing except nod, flash that pretty smile, and stay awake.

I replied to one of these ads because I was free that day, and the pay was decent for what was going to be a one-hour gig (1 million VND, equivalent to about US$45). You can eat for a week on that in Vietnam, if you go local.

The poster asked me to send a picture, and that I'd be selected if the company manager found me "attractive enough".

Apparently I didn't make the cut, because that was the last I heard from them. On the plus side, I was able to take

Tea Money

A businessman I spoke with reported that there's no way around paying tea money. If you want to keep doing business, there's no way around it. Just factor tea money into your budget.

"You learn quickly that it's hard to get paperwork done on time without paying an amount in excess of the filing fee," he said. The "excess fees", or tea money, are simply a way to get your paperwork to the top of the stack.

For example, an official may drop in at your office for a random inspection. He chats with you for a bit before asking to see some of your paperwork. "Hm, these two signatures don't match," the official will say, holding up two different forms.

You, the boss, know that they do actually match (because you signed them both)—but you don't point that out. You instead wrinkle your brow in confusion.

"There is a law that says they must match exactly before they are filed," the official will say. "But that's all right. You can just pay a fee, and then we will be able to file these forms for you."

And that's when you play ball and ask how much that fee will be. You'll be told a number.

Now, you don't just pull out your wallet and hand over some money. You dress up the proceedings a bit by procuring a fruit basket for the official and sending it to him. Inside the basket, you'll place an envelope of cash. Business has now been conducted, everyone's happy, and the world keeps on spinning.

my ugly mug down to the market and, for about a dollar, purchase and imbibe enough rice wine to help me forget this little ding to my ego.

TEACHING

There are two kinds of foreigners working in Vietnam: Those who teach English, and then maybe five other people (and who knows what they do?)

Guess which group I fall into?

We'll spend a little time on this one, because it's such a popular gig here.

As an English-speaking gun for hire I've worked a patchwork of jobs to keep gas in the motorbike. The ground is always shifting as classes start and then stop, but the relative lack of job stability is fine with me. It keeps my life from galvanizing into the ever-dreaded routine, and I get to meet and work with a veritable cross-section of the population.

At this particular period in history, native English speakers have a devastatingly easy path to a middle-class existence in Asia. Your path will become even smoother if you have a college degree (in literally any subject) and have a TEFL (Teaching English as a Foreign Language) certificate, or something equivalent to it.

But I know people here who speak English as a second (or third) language and haven't gone to university, and yet have still managed to put together a full slate of teaching hours.

Currently, the demand is such that there's always work, if you want it. Vietnam today is a place where every city block seems to have been colonized by a language centre. Centres usually pay in cash (usually by the month, but weekly is possible, too), under the table, with taxes already deducted.

Also, work hours can be erratic—you might be teaching at 9:15 on Friday night, while everyone you've ever met is out having the time of their lives—but that's the downside to escaping the much-ballyhooed structure of a nine-to-five.

You can live OK on a freelance teacher's earnings, but you should have an emergency fund saved up. Unless you're working on a long-term contract at an international school or some such, don't bank on receiving benefits, a housing allowance, or any of those other nice perks. Here in the Wild Wild East, it's all about personal responsibility. You fend for yourself.

Getting Into the Classroom
My story is a carbon copy of most foreign teacher's—I found a steady gig by posting on a Facebook jobs page. The owner

of the centre then messaged me, and I went in for a meeting. I expected a battery of traditional interview questions, but I was only asked one of any consequence: "When can you start?"

As I mentioned in Chapter 4, teaching skills and experience run a distant second to your appearance. Do you look like what Vietnamese think a native English speaker should look like? Then you're all set.

They might also ask you to do a 10-minute demo class on the spot. I once went in to see a recruiter and he asked me to model a short lesson for five year-old students. I made a show of looking around at the empty office we were sitting in.

"All right, sure. So where are the students?" I asked.

"I am the student," the recruiter said, and then he, a 40-year-old man in a tie, sat cross-legged on the floor and adopted a falsetto voice as he channelled a hyper child for the next 10 minutes.

Most places won't give you the shaft, and you'll get your money on time. But being that there are a few rotten apples in every bushel, try to talk to someone who's taught there previously. There are a few Facebook groups specifically devoted to this informal vetting practice.

A list of bigger English academies here includes Apax English, Language Link, ILA Vietnam, Apollo English, Cleverlearn, and so, so many more.

Private tutoring is an option, too. These gigs will usually come to you by word-of-mouth. If you do well with your students, then your client base will spread along with your legend. If you want to browse the classifieds for some teaching hours, start with these:

- **Tnhvietnam.com** (The New Hanoian — but it's not limited to Hanoi.)
- **Vietnamworks.com**

The ESL industry here is still as informal and unregulated as can be. But globalization and widespread English proficiency are coming, so easy employment won't last forever. Act now while supplies last.

Going Legit

Now, just because jobs tend to fall into your lap here doesn't mean they're all easy to get. I went into my first interview at an Australian-run center in Hanoi without an iota of preparation. Secure in my few years of prior experience, I thought it would be a layup, and privately expected an offer on the spot.

My hubris became my downfall; the instructors spent the next hour drilling me on the complexities of language teaching methodology, and threw a fusillade of situational hypotheticals my way. I didn't get the job.

Usually, that's how it'll shake out if you're trying to get hired at a high-paying center. And since those place are above board, they'll want to see original copies of your diploma and other documentation, so bring those with you. In general, it's best just to have as many of those on hand as possible in case they put you on a contract and level you up to a work permit.

So, this info so far has covered private centers. Public schools are another matter. The application process for those goes through the government and is more exhaustive, but you'll have the security of a contract, work permit and set (normal) work hours.

More information on the specific types of teaching jobs available in Vietnam are at www.gooverseas.com/teach-abroad/vietnam

VOLUNTEERING

I guess this one still counts as "work", even though the money is flowing in the opposite direction. I say this because most volunteer programs require a fee, which might or might not cover your accommodations and meals.

But there are enough programs out there that you should have no trouble enlisting with one. You can be here helping out for as long as six months or as little as a week, or even just an afternoon. Volunteers can be deployed in hospitals, rural schools, soup kitchens, and orphanages—but from what I understand, you usually have your choice of location.

For a summary of Vietnamese volunteer programs, go to www.gooverseas.com/volunteer-abroad/vietnam

NGOs

A lot of these programs have an intake process akin to volunteer organizations (though they may be more selective, due the lustre of the NGO label). Depending on your qualifications and the organization you join, you may have to pay a fee to the organization while you're working in Vietnam, or you might draw a small salary. If you don't find a programme to your liking—keep looking. There are scores of them.

Local NGOS commonly contribute assistance to fund-raising and welfare efforts. Beyond that, they'll work on human trafficking, educational and medical initiatives.

Several of my friends work at an NGO in Hanoi, but in an unpaid capacity. They've arranged some after-hours English tutoring to supplement their, well, nonexistent income.

To get started, go to www.ngocentre.org.vn/jobs

...And Everything Else

If you're here with some money saved up and are looking for some miscellaneous pursuits to fill the hours with, keep your eyes and ears open.

I know a few expats here who have managed to eke out some kind of an income doing freelance modelling and video shoots. As with teaching, most of these gigs come from the informal job fair that is Facebook. Models are hired for underwear or sportswear ads usually based on the few photos sent to the casting agent—no formal experience needed.

There was recently a local shoot for a Vietnamese war movie, and the production was seeking Western men to play wounded soldiers. The pay was 1 million VND per day, but I couldn't take the job, due to my teaching hours.

Some people have a fantasy of coming over and working in a coffee shop or something while they write poems about travelling. But unless you're gallivanting on a trust fund, that's a surefire path to homelessness; the pay scale for those jobs is local (think 20,000–30,000 VND an hour).

CHAPTER 10

FAST FACTS

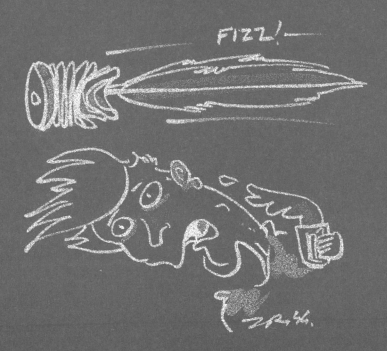

> ❝Get your facts first, then you can
> distort them as you please.❞

> — **Mark Twain, writer**

Official Name
Socialist Republic of Vietnam

Capital
Hanoi

Flag
Red background with a yellow star in the center

Motto
Doc lap — Tu do — Hanh phuc
(Independence — Freedom — Happiness)

National Anthem
Tien Quan Ca (Army March)

Time
Indochina Time (UTC + 7)

Telephone Country Code
+84

Land
Vietnam is a long, thin strip of land that begins at the southern border of China and terminates between the Gulf of Thailand and the South China Sea. It's bordered by Laos and Cambodia to the west.

Area
Total: 331,210 sq km (127,880 sq miles)
Land: 310,070 sq km (119,718 sq miles)
Water: 21,140 sq km (8,162 sq miles)

Highest Point
Mount Fansipan (3,143 m / 10, 312 ft)

Climate
Ranges from monsoonal in the North to tropical in the South. Hot and rainy from May to September; warm and dry from October to March.

Population
91,700,000 (as of 2015). Vietnam is the 14th most-populous nation in the world, and the 8th most-populous in Asia. As of 2016, the population is growing at 0.95% annually.

Ethnic Groups
The Kinh (Viet) make up 85% of the population. Tay, Khmer, Thai, Muong, Nung and Hoa groups mainly comprise the remainder.

Religion
Primarily Buddhism, Caodaism and Catholism

Languages and Dialects
Vietnamese is the national official language (surprise), with regional dialects used outside the cities. English is a widely-spoken second language, and there's also a limited presence of French, Mandarin Chinese and Khmer.

Government Type
Communist state (more specifically, it's a Unitary Marxist-Leninist one-party state)

Head of State
- Nguyen Phu Trong (general secretary of the Communist Party — the most powerful person in Vietnam),
- Nguyen Xuan Phuc (prime minister),
- Tran Dai Quang (president, position largely ceremonial).

Administrative Divisions
58 provinces, along with five state-run municipalities

Major Cities
Hanoi, Ho Chi Minh City, Haiphong, Danang and Hue

Currency
Vietnamese dong (VND)

Gross Domestic Product (GDP)
US$ 593.509 billion (US$6,414 per capital) — 2015 estimate, based on PPP

Agricultural Products
Cashews, coffee, black pepper and rice

Other Products
Tea, rubber, fish and seafood

Industries
Food processing, bauxite mining, garments, shoes, machine-building and mobile phones

Exports
Clothing, textiles, shoes, electronics, coffee, rice and seafood

Imports
Machinery, computers, textiles, telephones and petroleum

Ports and Harbours
Ho Chi Minh City, Danang, Haiphong, Hanoi, Na Ngoi, Can Tho, Hon Gay, My Tho, Nghe Tinh, Phu My, Tan Cang, Vung Tau, Campha, Dai Hung, Dong Thap, Hon Chong, Le Mon, Nam Can, Nha Trang, Quy Nhon and Van Phong Bay

Airports
As of 2017, the country has about 25 civilian airports. The Big Three are:

- Noi Bai International—Serves Hanoi and the North.
- Tan Son Nhat International—Your Saigon airport option. It's a war relic and is scheduled to be replaced by Long Than International Airport in 2025. The new airport will be designed to process 100 million passengers a year.
- Da Nang International—This will drop you into the country's approximate midpoint.

FAMOUS PEOPLE
- **Dinh La Thang:** The secretary of the Ho Chi Minh City Party Committee since early 2016. He's known for his policies to improve the city. Even in the North, he's the first name many locals give you when discussing famous politicians.
- **Son Tung M-TP:** This young man is a singer-songwriter, and after listening to a few of his tracks, I guess you

could call him the Justin Bieber of Vietnam. Even if EDM (electronic dance music) or pop isn't your thing, you'll still see the guy all over the place; his face been pasted on flat surfaces all over the country in fulfilment of the endorsement deals he's signed.

- **My Tam:** She's a musician and pop singer with a three-octave vocal range. Her long run of success began in 1999, and she was regarded for a time as the "Queen of V-Pop". She has served as a judge on the TV shows Vietnam Idol and The Voice of Vietnam.
- **Ho Ngoc Ha:** Another songstress who performs ballads, pop and R&B. Like her fellow luminary My Tam, she has also put in judge time on the music show circuit. Outside of her musical output, she is known for her fashion sense and charity work—and her romantic life gets a little attention as well.
- **Xuan Bac:** A comedian and actor who has also hosted a few TV game shows. He has also served as a UNICEF Goodwill Ambassador, and in that capacity raised awareness about the need for water sanitation in rural Vietnam.
- **Le Cong Vinh:** A footballer who, since 2015, has taken the field as a striker for the Becamex Binh Duong Team. He also plays for the Vietnamese national team, which has allowed him to do damage on the international circuit, scoring clutch goals that knocked nations such as Thailand, Singapore and the United Arab Emirates out of regional tournaments.
- **Hoang Xuan Vinh:** An army colonel and sports shooter who became an instant national hero after his showing in the 2016 Summer Games in Rio, where he won a gold medal for his shooting in the 10-metre air

pistol event. A few days later, he become a two-time Olympian when he shot his way to a silver medal in the 50-metre event.

PLACES OF INTEREST IN HANOI

Ho Chi Minh's Mausoleum

A granite structure that is the memorial and final resting place of Uncle Ho. It's placed in the city's Ba Dinh Square, where Ho proclaimed Vietnamese independence in 1945. A long line of visitors queue up each day to observe Ho's preserved body. Long pants must be worn by both men and women, and there's no photography allowed inside.

You can also visit the nearby Ho Chi Minh Museum after you see the mausoleum. It walks you through Uncle Ho's life, from his birth, to his world travels in his pursuit of independence, all the way up to his death in the midst of the war.

Temple of Literature

A thousand-year-old temple complex in Ba Dinh District constructed to honour Confucius and the Vietnamese scholars he inspired. It is a shrine both to their contributions to the ancient Imperial Academy and to the pursuit of knowledge itself. The temple spread is made up of five courtyards, separated by handsome gateways, and screened off from the rumble of the city by rows of trees. If you've procured any Vietnamese cash yet, then you've already seen the temple—it's on the back of the 100,000 dong note.

The Old Quarter

Probably Hanoi's biggest selling point. The Old Quarter is a honeycomb of a few dozen shadowy streets, and is a mystical, exotic refuge from the bland grayness that defines the rest of the city. It has Buddhist temples set up right next to quiet hotels, colonial French buildings and about a million street restaurants and cafés. The Old Quarter generally resists the change that morphs the world around it.

It's the part of the city foreigners have been gravitating to for 2,000 years — it played host to the Chinese before it did the French, and it's currently under siege by backpackers. On Friday, Saturday and Sunday nights, the streets are blocked off and vendors fill the lanes for the Night Market.

Hoan Kiem Lake

On the edge of Hanoi's Old Quarter you'll find an oval-shaped lake. There's a tiny tower on an island at the southern end of it, and a temple stands on a larger island in the North.

Legend has it that Vietnamese Emperor Le Loi was gifted a sword by the gods in order to fight off the nation's Chinese rulers. One day when he was on the lake, he was asked by the Golden Turtle God to return his sword to the deities by throwing it into the water. He obeyed.

Floodlights keep the area sparkling after dark. On Friday, Saturday and Sunday nights the road around the lake is closed to vehicles and turned into a walking street, in tandem with the Old Quarter's Night Market.

Hoa Lo Prison

Built by the French to jail Vietnamese dissidents, it was later repurposed by the North Vietnamese as a wartime prison.

The French called it Maison Centrale and later American POWs dryly nicknamed it "The Hanoi Hilton". It's now been mostly demolished, but the gateway area still remains, and there's a museum attached to it.

Ho Tay

This translates to "West Lake" and the district on its northern shore is where most of the expats live—they refer to it as Tay Ho.

West Lake is on this list because everyone should, at least once, do a motorbike cruise of the 17km road that brackets it. Bring your camera.

Tran Quoc Pagoda

A 1,400-year-old Buddhist pagoda on a lush little island just off the shore of West Lake. The pagoda is quite tall, and has Buddha statues laid into it. Visitors come to the temple grounds to burn incense and leave offerings, and monks live on the island to this day.

On a related note, US military history buffs should leave the pagoda after they're done touring and make their way cross Thanh Nien Road, which separates West Lake from another smaller lake, called Truc Bach.

That's the lake where US Navy pilot (and future politician) John McCain was shot down during a bombing raid in 1967, and a monument marks the spot where he was dragged out the water.

The Military History Museum

This museum is two traffic lights from Ho Chi Minh's Mausoleum, and directly across the street from a statue of Russian comrade Vladimir Lenin. Captured American warplanes and ordnance are piled up in the courtyard between the museum building and the 41m-tall Flag Tower, a 200-year-old observation post.

It's an older museum, and not all the captions on the exhibits are in English—but it's worth an afternoon, if only to view Vietnam's long history of conflict from their own vantage point.

The Women's Museum

Just a few blocks away from Hoan Kiem Lake, this museum has four floors of exhibitions that illustrate the role of women in Vietnamese society — past and present, urban and rural. There's a section devoted to the women's wholehearted involvement in the war effort via espionage and guerilla warfare, as well as a close look at Vietnam's countryside wedding customs and family life.

The Museum of Ethnography

This museum, in the Cau Giay District, is bit of a jump away from downtown. It takes the wide view of the Vietnamese cultural make-up by focusing on all 54 of its ethnic groups. They're all represented, whether it be with artefacts, artwork, or reconstructions of tribal homes.

PLACES OF INTEREST IN SAIGON

Ben Thanh Market

A huge indoor bazaar packed with hundreds of stalls and vendors. After walking through it, I'm having trouble thinking of anything you can't buy there. It's in District 1, and is one of the city's defining landmarks.

War Remnants Museum

Located in District 3, but it's walkable from District 1 (where most of the tourist magnets are). With its captured weaponry on display outside, this museum is similar to its Hanoian counterpart, the Military History Museum. However, this one is maintains a singular focus on the "American War".

The museum traces the conflict from its earliest catalyst, then through the mad carnage of the fighting itself, then all the way up to the postwar consequences Vietnam is still grappling with. Keep in mind that the photo exhibitions are extremely, unflinchingly graphic.

Independence Palace

The workplace of the South Vietnamese President during the war — and also the site of the war's dramatic denouement, when a North Vietnamese battle tank bashed through the palace gates, allowing Norther officers to receive the South's surrender in person. You can tour the offices and war rooms inside the palace.

Surrounded by towering trees and parks the size of football fields, the palace is located in District 1. It's also known as Reunification Palace.

Saigon Notre-Dame Basilica

This huge Catholic Cathedral was installed by the French in the 19th century. The tiles and red bricks used in its construction were imported from Europe, and then the structure was assembled in Saigon's District 1. The cathedral is peaked by twin bell towers, and a statue of the Virgin Mary stands in the square out front. Admission is free.

Bitexco Financial Tower

At 68 storeys, it's the tallest building in Saigon, and the first ultra-modern addition to its skyline. Sleek and curvy (and with a helipad to boot) it's a symbol of Southern ambition. Killer views are on offer from the Saigon Skydeck on the 49th storey.

Ho Chi Minh City Hall

Built by the French in 1908, this building looks more like a royal palace than it does a city hall. It's closed to the public, but the photo ops outside are good enough that you wouldn't want to go inside a stuffy old building anyway.

A seemingly endless courtyard in front of the hall stretches all the way out to the Saigon River. There's also a 7m-tall bronze statue of Ho Chi Minh himself in front of the hall, one arm raised, greeting both the people below him and the shiny buildings rising up to the side.

Cu Chi Tunnels

Another must-see for war historians, the Cu Chi tunnels are only a small fraction of the huge subterranean network employed during battle by the Viet Cong for shelter, transportation and storage. A tunnel tour immerses you in the claustrophobia, darkness and booby traps that were features of this particularly hellish battlefront. You can also fire off a few rounds from an AK-47 at the shooting range.

The tunnels are about an hour away from the city centre.

CULTURE QUIZ

SITUATION 1

You're a week into your new job and, in an effort to get to know a co-worker, you invite him out for lunch. When the check is dropped, you pull out your wallet to pay for your meal, but your co-worker makes no move to do the same. What's your play?

Ⓐ Feign polite confusion and say something to the effect of, "Right, and I think your dish cost 30,000 dong."

Ⓑ Drop a hint by counting out your share and putting your money on the table.

Ⓒ Make a show of pulling up the calculator on your smartphone and subtracting your meal from the total on the bill.

Ⓓ Pay the entire check and return to the office.

Comment

In the West, our mealtime customs are less ironclad. But in Vietnamese culture it's expected that the person who did the invitation will treat their guest to the meal. And in return, a reciprocal meal (or coffee, or drink) is usually scheduled.

So the right answer is **O**.

A, **B** and **C** may work back at home. But this is Vietnam, and, as they say, you're not in Kansas anymore.

SITUATION 2

The next morning, you're in the crowded lobby of your office building, waiting to catch the elevator. That's when a grandmother, carrying her grandchild, blatantly shuffles in front of you and essentially robs you of a spot in the next car. How do you react?

A Heave out a gale-force sigh and stomp up the stairs, hoping you can hike up to your desk on time.

B Give her the benefit of the doubt by tapping her on the shoulder, then politely motioning that she should move behind you.

C Glance at the other people in the area and shrug, but ultimately bite the bullet and stay where you are.

O Quietly but firmly reclaim your spot by moving in front of her.

Comment

Well, **A** is a little rude, and there are enough rude foreigners here already. (And do you really want to climb all those steps?) And while **B** and **O** are tempting options, **C** is probably best.

As an older Vietnamese person, the grandmother carries status that you, a (probably) younger foreigner, do not. Then there's the fact that she's caring for a child. She's probably used to getting a pass in such situations, and it would be rude to challenge her while she's on kid duty.

And if she's not carrying a child? Let her cut anyway.

Keep in mind that you are going to get cut in line. The Vietnamese seem to have a Darwinian, blatant attitude about such activity. If they can get away with it, they'll probably try it. After all, they get practice all day; traffic is essentially a mass exercise in ego assertion via angling around others to cut them off.

SITUATION 3

One evening a coworker sends you a Facebook message. A colleague has invited you out to a dinner, along with everyone else in the office, this coming Saturday night. The problem? You already have plans to attend an expat friend's birthday party on the same night. What's the solution?

Ⓐ Take up your colleague's invite, and message your friend saying that you'll have to miss most of the party due to a work dinner.

Ⓑ Tell your colleague that you unfortunately already have very important plans that night. Follow this by profusely apologizing to him both over Facebook (with a superfluous amount of crying emojis) and in person at the office.

Ⓒ Resign from your position—thereby forfeiting your work permit—out of loyalty to your friend.

Ⓓ Attend the work dinner for a polite amount of time, then cut out a little early and head to your friend's party.

Comment

We have a few winners—it all depends on your objectives here.

If you're still new to the job and intend to cement your business relationships, **Ⓐ** is a wise (if unappealing) play.

Choosing this means you buy the ticket and take the ride, and should attend the dinner (and whatever post-meal shenanigans the group settles on) to completion, which pretty much rules out **D**.

Rejecting someone's invitation will cause them to lose face, so while **B** is an appealing option that lets you off the hook, it might embarrass your colleague or create a little distance between you.

If you've known your colleague for longer, and already have good rapport with them? Go to your friend's party, or go for **D** by splitting the difference and hitting up both gatherings. Your colleagues should understand. Work matters here, but it's generally not expected to be your religion (as is the case in Japan and South Korea).

And **C**? That was a joke—don't do that.

SITUATION 4

The next day, you're back at work. You realize that a Vietnamese worker you oversee has, in a rush, completed the wrong paperwork. Said worker is new to the company, is still learning the ropes, and is worried about keeping his job. At a staff meeting, your boss asks you who's at fault. How do you respond?

A Put on a show of absolute confusion and say you hadn't realized that any paperwork needed to be done.

B Inform your boss that your worker was at fault, while at the same time coming to his defence by stating that his mistake was an honest one.

C Take the hit for your worker by claiming the mistake was actually your own, because you assigned him the wrong paperwork. Then tell your boss you'll file the correct forms immediately.

⊙ Tell a little white lie and say that you're not exactly sure where the fault lies, but you'll correct the error right away.

Comment

Answer **Ⓐ** could paint you as unprepared and irresponsible. And while you don't probably value face in the way that the Vietnamese do, you might lose a little standing in their eyes (and your boss's).

Ⓑ is the most wrong answer, because it puts your colleague straight in the boss's cross-hairs, which is a mortifying place for a Vietnamese subordinate to be.

So, while it shades on the side of dishonesty, I would probably choose **Ⓒ** and tell a diplomatic fib in order to help my worker save face. The way I see it, I have a little more face to lose than the Vietnamese do.

Why not **Ⓓ**? It's probably too dishonest, and also makes you seem incapable of running your team.

Do enough time in 'Nam, and you'll acquire the situational finesse necessary to keep others out from under the bus wheels.

SITUATION 5

You're granted a two-week reprieve from the workplace as Vietnam celebrates Tet. When you return to work, your cheeks are a little puffy from some extra vacation brews. A Vietnamese colleague sees you at your desk on Monday and says, "Welcome back! Oh, you have gotten fat!"

How do you deal with this?

Ⓐ Pretend you didn't hear what she said, sit down and get to work.

Ⓑ Jab back! Laughingly tell your colleague that you think she's gotten fat, too.

◉ Nod and then tell your colleague that, where you're from, what she just said is considered rude—just so that she's aware of your cultural policy on such comments.

◉ Hold your tongue as you absorb the hit, then chuckle and say something like, "Hey, you're probably right—I enjoyed myself on vacation." (Then go to the gym after work.)

Comment

Things like this will happen. You might remember this from Chapter 9, but people think nothing of being forthright in Vietnam.

So, **◉** isn't a good option because your colleague will probably sense that you're ignoring her, but she probably won't understand why—and you'll come off as rude and detached.

◉ probably won't work, either. Since it'll be a reflex dig, you might seem spiteful while you're saying it (and Vietnamese people don't really seem to ever gain weight, so it won't be true, anyway.)

And as for **◉**—well, it doesn't really matter how they do things where you're from, because this is Vietnam.

So we're down to **◉**.

I'm told in short order when a new haircut doesn't look as good as the old one or that I look like a "raccoon" if I have dark circles under my eyes. Personal questions ("Why aren't you married yet?") and flat-out rude statements ("I think you're here because you are not intelligent enough to get a job in America") are absolutely fair game.

Now, honesty has a silver lining; if you're starting to gain a few, at least you'll be made aware of this immediately.

DOS AND DON'TS

DO

- Attempt to learn, at the very least, pleasantries in Vietnamese.
- Remove your shoes before entering a Vietnamese home or business.
- Greet the eldest person (with a short bow) in a group situation before greeting anyone else.
- Defer to the middle-aged or elderly (even if they cut you in line).
- Pay for someone's meal or drink if you've invited them out (they'll pay for your food if they're the one who invited you out).
- Bring friends and close colleagues small gifts after travelling somewhere.
- Bring a small cash gift to a wedding, engagement party or funeral.
- For survival's sake, honk your bike or car horn at every intersection.
- Keep close track of your arrival date into the country so you won't overstay your visa.
- Lock your bike and keep your possessions secured whenever you're in public.

DON'T

- Embarrass someone by pointing out an error or mistake in public.
- Show overt amounts of affection in public.
- Point at someone with your index finger, or beckon them over to you with a "come here gesture".
- Reject someone's social invitation (unless you have a bulletproof excuse for doing so).
- Take the last piece of food from a group dish while eating with others.
- Stick your chopsticks straight into a bowl of food (such that they're standing vertically). Instead, lay them flat atop your bowl.
- Speak ill of the government or Ho Chi Minh among mixed company.
- Display offense or inform a Vietnamese person you think they're rude when asked a personal question.
- Angrily confront vendors or taxi drivers if you're scammed.

GLOSSARY

In case you haven't come yet across a shortlist of Vietnamese survival phrases, I've put one here. This should keep you busy for a day or two. Or a month or two, depending on your academic track record. If you see me out in Hanoi (I like to eat at the Quong Ba flower market) then there will be a pop quiz.

Sounding them out phonetically might work—but even if you manage the right pronunciation, you might be getting (read: absolutely will be getting) the wrong tone. Again, YouTube is your friend. When words fail (and they will), try miming. Warm up with a few rounds of Charades before you get on the plane.

Vietnamese	English
Xin chào (sin chow)	Hello. (In a more casual setting you can just say "chao".)
Tạm biệt (tam byet)	Good-bye.
Tôi tên là _____ (toy ten la)	My name is _____.
Cảm ơn (gauhm uhhn)	Thank you.
Khỏe không? (kweh khong?)	How are you?
Khoẻ, cảm ơn (kweh, gauhm uhhn)	Fine, thanks.
Xin lỗi (sin loy)	I'm sorry. (You may or may not hear this in traffic, right after someone crashes their bike into you.)
Không sao (khong sow)	No problem.

Tôi không hiểu (toy khong he-ew)	I don't understand.
Giá bao nhiêu? (zia bow ne-ew)	How much is it?
_____ ở đâu? (oh zow)	Where is _____(thing)?*

*Placing another word before "ở đâu?" is how you ask where that thing is. Depending on the fluency of your conversation partner, you might be able to hack your languages together and say something like "**Bathroom** ở đâu?"

NUMBERS

–	Zero
Một	One
Hai	Two
Ba	Three
Bốn	Four
Năm	Five
Sáu	Six
Bảy	Seven
Tám	Eight
Chín	Nine
Mười	Ten

RESOURCE GUIDE

EMERGENCY PHONE NUMBERS
- **110**: International Operator
- **113**: Police
- **114**: Fire
- **115**: Ambulance

MAKING PHONE CALLS
If you're calling a Vietnamese phone number from outside the country, make sure you include the country code (+84) at the start of the number. To dial within Vietnam, you drop the country code and substitute in a "0." So, the phone number (+84) 9 03XX XXXX then becomes 09 03XX XXXX.

EMBASSIES
A list of 94 foreign embassies and consulates in Vietnam can be found at:

http://embassy.goabroad.com/embassies-in/vietnam

HOSPITALS & CLINICS
Hanoi
- **French Hospital of Hanoi**
  1 Phuong Mai, Dong Da, Hanoi
  Phone: (84 4) 3577 1100
- **Hanoi Medical University Hospital**
  1 Ton That Tung, Trung Tu, Dong Da, Hanoi
  Phone: (84 4) 3574 7788
- **Hong Ngoc Hospital**
  55 Yen Ninh, Truc Bach, Ba Dinh, Hanoi
  Phone: (84 4) 3927 5568

- **Family Medical Practice — Hanoi**
  298l Kim Ma, Ba Dinh, Hanoi
  Phone: (84 4) 3843 0748
- **International SOS Clinic**
  51 Xuan Dieu, Quang An, Tay Ho, Hanoi
  Phone: (84 4) 3934 0666

Saigon
- **Hanh Phuc International Hospital**
  97 Nguyen Thi Minh Khai Street, District 1, Ho Chi Minh City
  Phone: (84 8) 3925 9797
- **FV (Franco-Vietnamese) Hospital**
  6 Nguyen Luong Bang, District 7, Ho Chi Minh City
  Phone: (84 8) 5411 3333
- **Columbia Asia International Clinic — Saigon**
  8 Alexandre de Rhodes, District 1, Ho Chi Minh City
  Phone: (84 8) 3823 8888
- **Family Medical Practice — Ho Chi Minh City**
  34 Le Duan, Ben Nghe, District 1, Ho Chi Minh City
  Phone: (84 8) 3822 7848

SCHOOLS
Hanoi
- **United Nations International School of Hanoi**
  www.unishanoi.org
  Phone: (84 4) 3758 1551
  Email: info@unishanoi.org
- **Hanoi International School**
  www.hisvietnam.com
  Phone: (84 4) 3832 7379
  Email: contact form on website

- **British International School**
  www.nordangliaeducation.com/our-schools/vietnam/
  hanoi/bis
  Phone: (84 4) 3946 0435
  Email: bishanoi@bishanoi.com
  (This school also maintains a branch in Saigon.)
- **St Paul American School Hanoi**
  www.stpaulhanoi.com.vn
  Phone: (84 4) 3399 6464
  Email: info@stpaulhanoi.com
- **Hanoi International Kindergarten**
  http://hik.edu.vn/
  Phone: (84 4) 3719 1248

Saigon
- **International School Ho Chi Minh City**
  www.ishcmc.com
  Phone: (84 8) 3898 9100
  Email: admissions@ishcmc.edu.vn
- **Singapore International School**
  www.sis.edu.vn
  Phone: (84 8) 5431 7477 (Saigon South campus)
  Email: contact form on website
  (The school has 15 campuses across Vietnam.)
- **South Saigon International School**
  www.ssis.edu.vn
  Phone: (84 8) 5413 0901
  Email: admissions@ssis.edu.vn
- **The American School of Vietnam**
  www.theamericanschool.edu.vn
  Phone: (84 8) 3 519 2223
  Email: contact form on website

- **The Canadian International School**
  www.cis.edu.vn
  Phone: (84 8) 5412 3456
  Email: cis.edu.vn
- **The Australian School of Vietnam**
  www.aisvietnam.com
  Phone: (84 8) 3742 4040
  Email: enrolments@aisvietnam.com
- **Saigon Montessori International Kindergarten**
  www.smisvn.com
  Phone: (84 8) 5412 4772
  Email: smik.edu@gmail.com
- **Saigon Kids Kindergarten**
  www.saigonkidskindergarten.com
  Phone: (84 8) 3740 8081
  Email: saigonkidscentre@yahoo.com

LANGUAGE SCHOOLS
Hanoi
- **Hidden Hanoi**
  www.hiddenhanoi.com.vn/language-school123Vietnamese
  www.123vietnamese.com

Saigon
- **Saigon Language School**
  saigonlanguage.com/en/
- **Vietnamese Language Studies**
  www.vlstudies.com

EXPAT CLUBS

- **The American Club Hanoi**
  21 Hai Ba Trung, Hoan Kiem District
  www.business-in-asia.com/americanclub.html
- **Internations**
  www.internations.org/vietnam-expats
- **Expat Arrivals**
  www.expatarrivals.com/vietnam/moving-to-vietnam
- **Expat Exchange**
  www.expatexchange.com/vietnam/liveinvietnam.html
- **International Ladies in Vietnam**
  www.ilvietnam.com
- **Expat Women Vietnam**
  www.expatwoman.com/vietnam

RELIGIOUS INSTITUTIONS

- **Vietnamese Buddhist Association**
  www.chuaquansu.net
  This is the website of Quan Su Temple, where the association is headquartered (it's in Hanoi's Hoan Kiem District). The website appears to be in Vietnamese only, so a personal visit may be in order.
- **Islam in Vietnam**
  A list of five major mosques in Vietnam can be found here: www.vietnamvisa-easy.com/blog/islamic-mosques-in-vietnam/
- **Chabad of Vietnam** (Saigon-based)
  www.jewishvietnam.com
- **Vietnamese Catholic Church**
  A directory of Vietnam's Catholic Dioceses is on offer from the Union of Catholic Asian News's database at: http://directory.ucanews.com/country/vietnam/34

- **Mission Vietnam (Christian Missions Organization)**
  www.missionvietnam.org

VOLUNTEER ORGANIZATIONS
- **International Volunteer HQ**
  www.volunteerhq.org/volunteer-in-vietnam-ho-chi-minh
- **Vina Volunteer Service**
  http://vietnamvolunteer.net
- **Volunteering Solutions**
  www.volunteeringsolutions.com/volunteer-in-vietnam
- **Projects Abroad**
  www.projects-abroad.org/volunteer-destinations/
  volunteer-vietnam
- **Globe Aware**
  www.globeaware.org/destinations/asia/vietnam

BOOKSHOPS
Hanoi
- **Bookworm**
  44 Chau Long, Ba Dinh District, Ho Chi Minh City
- **Fahasa Bookstore**
  338 Xa Dan, Dong Da District, Ho Chi Minh City
- And check out "**Book Street**", where there's a few
  shops that have English books. Its Vietnamese name is
  Đinh Lễ, and it's in Hoan Kiem District.

Saigon
- **BOA Bookstore**
  6 Cong Truong Quoc Te, Building C19, 3rd Floor,
  District 3, Ho Chi Minh City
  (It's hidden away like the doorway to Narnia—ask
  someone in the cafés nearby exactly how to get there).

- **Book Cafe PNC**
  105 Tran Hung Dao, District 5, Ho Chi Minh City
- **Fahasa Bookstore**
  (Fahasa has over a dozen branches in Saigon — Google which one is nearest you.)

NEWSPAPERS
- The Saigon Times (daily newspaper)
- Vietnam News (the national English daily — online & print editions)
- Tuoitrenews.vn (daily online English newspaper)

MAGAZINES
- The Word Vietnam
- Asia Life Vietnam
- Oi Vietnam

All magazines are available both online and in print.

FURTHER READING

NON-FICTION

The Rough Guide to Vietnam, Rough Guides, London: Rough Guides Press, 2015.

National Geographic Traveler: Vietnam, 3rd Edition, James Sullivan, Des Moines: National Geographic, 2015.

Vietnam—Culture Smart! The Essential Guide to Customs & Culture, Geoffrey Murray, London: Kuperard, 2016.

Vietnamese Home Cooking, Charles Phan, New York: Ten Speed Press, 2012.

It's a Living: Work and Life in Vietnam Today, Gerard Sasges, Singapore: National University of Singapore Press, 2013.

Vietnam: A New History, Christopher Goscha, New York: Basic Books, 2016.

Vietnam: Rising Dragon, Bill Hayton, New Haven: Yale University Press, 2011.

The Killing Zone: My Life in the Vietnam War, Frederick Downs, Jr., New York: W.W. Norton & Company, 2007.

FICTION

The Things They Carried, Tim O'Brien, New York: Mariner Books, 2009.

Matterhorn: A Novel of the Vietnam War, Karl Marlantes, New York: Grove Press, 2011.

The Sympathizer: A Novel, Viet Thanh Nguyen, New York: Grove Press, 2016.

ABOUT THE AUTHOR

Ben Engelbach is an American who was born and raised in New Hampshire. He studied screenwriting at Biola University in La Mirada, California, and upon graduation fled East in order to dodge the Great Recession. Finding Asia an agreeable travel destination, he stuck around, teaching English in both China and South Korea before heading to Vietnam in 2016. He currently lives in Hanoi and *CultureShock! Vietnam* is his first book.

INDEX

Titles in the **CultureShock!** series:

For more information about any of these titles, please contact the Publisher via email at: genref@sg.marshallcavendish.com or visit our website at: www.marshallcavendish.com/genref